LEARNING TO READ

Unwin Education Books

Education Since 1800   IVOR MORRISH
Physical Education for Teaching   BARBARA CHURCHER
Organising and Integrating the Infant Day   JOY TAYLOR
The Philosophy of Education: An Introduction   HARRY SCHOFIELD
Assessment and Testing: An Introduction   HARRY SCHOFIELD
Education: Its Nature and Purpose   M. V. C. JEFFREYS
Learning in the Primary School   KENNETH HASLAM
The Sociology of Education: An Introduction   IVOR MORRISH
Developing a Curriculum   AUDREY and HOWARD NICHOLLS
Teacher Education and Cultural Change   H. DUDLEY PLUNKETT and
   JAMES LYNCH
Reading and Writing in the First School   JOY TAYLOR
Approaches to Drama   DAVID A. MALE
Aspects of Learning   BRIAN O'CONNELL
Focus on Meaning   JOAN TOUGH
Moral Education   WILLIAM KAY
Concepts in Primary Education   JOHN E. SADLER
Moral Philosophy for Education   ROBIN BARROW
Principles of Classroom Learning and Perception   RICHARD J. MUELLER
Education and the Community   ERIC MIDWINTER
Creative Teaching   AUDREY and HOWARD NICHOLLS
The Preachers of Culture   MARGARET MATHIESON
Mental Handicap: An Introduction   DAVID EDEN
Aspects of Educational Change   IVOR MORRISH
Beyond Initial Reading   JOHN POTTS
The Foundations of Maths in the Infant School   JOY TAYLOR
Common Sense and the Curriculum   ROBIN BARROW
The Second 'R'   WILLIAM HARPIN
The Diploma Disease   RONALD DORE
The Development of Meaning   JOAN TOUGH
The Place of Commonsense in Educational Thought   LIONEL ELVIN
Language in Teaching and Learning   HAZEL FRANCIS
Patterns of Education in the British Isles   NIGEL GRANT and ROBERT BELL
Philosophical Foundation for the Curriculum   ALLEN BRENT
World Faiths in Education   W. OWEN COLE
Classroom Language: What Sort?   JILL RICHARDS
Philosophy and Human Movement   DAVID BEST
Secondary Schools and the Welfare Network   DAPHNE JOHNSON *et al.*
Educating Adolescent Girls   J. M. CHANDLER
Classroom Observation of Primary School Children   RICHARD W. MILLS
Essays on Educators   R. S. PETERS
Comparative Education: Some Considerations of Method   BRIAN HOLMES
Education and the Individual   BRENDA COHEN
In-service Education within the School   ROLAND W. MORANT
Moral Development and Moral Education   R. S. PETERS
Learning to Read   HAZEL FRANCIS

Learning to Read

Literate behaviour and orthographic knowledge

by
HAZEL FRANCIS
Professor of Educational Psychology
University of London Institute of Education

London
GEORGE ALLEN & UNWIN
Boston   Sydney

George Allen & Unwin (Publishers) Ltd,
40 Museum Street, London WC1A 1LU, UK

George Allen & Unwin (Publishers) Ltd,
Park Lane, Hemel Hempstead, Herts HP2 4TE, UK

Allen & Unwin, Inc.,
9 Winchester Terrace, Winchester, Mass. 01890, USA

George Allen & Unwin Australia Pty Ltd,
8 Napier Street, North Sydney, NSW 2060, Australia

First published in 1982

British Library Cataloguing in Publication Data

Francis, Hazel
   Learning to read.
1. Reading
I. Title
428.4   LB1139.R4
ISBN 0-04-372037-4
ISBN 0-04-372038-2 Pbk

Library of Congress Cataloging in Publication Data

Francis, Hazel
   Learning to Read
   Includes Index.
I. Reading (Elementary) I. Title. II. Series.
LB1573.F65   372.4   82–6685
ISBN 0–04–372037–4   AACR2
ISBN 0–04–372038–2 (Pbk)

Set in 10 on 11 point Times by Rowland Phototypesetting Ltd,
Bury St Edmunds, Suffolk
and printed in Great Britain
by Billing and Sons Ltd, Guildford,
London and Worcester

Contents

Preface

In their book on deprivation and the infant school Chazan and Williams (1978) comment that very little is known of the development of early reading skills in individual children, and it seems to be true that few investigations of such learning have been reported. Much, on the other hand, has been written about methods of teaching, the design of reading material and the problems of older children with reading difficulties. The discrepancy is interesting for two reasons. First, it leaves a gap in information available to primary school teachers who are necessarily interested in the individual children in their charge; and secondly, it suggests a prevailing view that reading must be taught, and taught in such a way that children are required to be conscious of various strategies thought to help them 'break the code' that relates written to spoken language. Yet, just as in learning to talk, children do tend to go about tasks in their own way, often being quite unaware of the kind of information processing on which developing skill depends. Thus on starting school many children experience a kind of confrontation between informal learning strategies of their own and formal teaching strategies of the school. This book is an attempt to chart the reading progress of a sample of children in the first three years of schooling, paying special attention to the problems they encountered and the strategies they adopted. In their interests fictitious names have been used, and neither the school nor the education authority is identified.

The author is extremely grateful to various people who made the study possible. First, the chief education officer and his advisers, who gave consent to observation and who helped to locate a suitable school for it, must be warmly thanked. Educational research in schools carries ethical and practical hazards, and can be very worrying to the authorities concerned. Co-operation and support is invaluable and much appreciated. Secondly, the headmistress and staff who were willing to tolerate research observation in their school for such a long period must also be thanked. But, because they went far beyond toleration and were positively welcoming and helpful, the author knows no way of thanking them sufficiently for the way they shared their professional knowledge and were so willing to discuss the research as it progressed. Finally, the debt owed to the children is immense. Fortunately they seemed to enjoy what was involved. It is the author's sincere hope that the study will be found useful by at least some of those concerned to provide for, and to help with, the very early steps in such children's learning to read.

Chapter 1

Introduction: Problems in Learning to Read

This introductory chapter is not meant to be a comprehensive survey of research on learning to read, but to set the stage for the rest of the book. The very extensive literature on methods of teaching reading and on the development of learning materials is largely irrelevant, because the central question being explored here is what children understand and do in their earliest steps towards reading. An eclectic teaching context with no tightly controlled learning programme has been chosen as the setting. It might be claimed by enthusiasts of one programme or another that children would have learned more speedily or thoroughly under the different conditions they advocate; but such claims require testing, and this is a hazardous enterprise not attempted here. What will be done is to emphasise two aspects of learning which are not clearly brought out in the literature on early steps in reading, but which will be traced in the case studies reported in the rest of the book. They are learning the significance of the acts of reading and writing and gaining incidental knowledge of the orthographic structure, that is, the spelling system, of written English. In attending to these it is not suggested that perceptual-motor skills, motivation, knowing about reading behaviour and relating script to spoken English are not important, but simply that they have hitherto received more attention, possibly because they seem to be more obviously related to past and current schemes of teaching reading and to assessment of 'readiness' and reading skills.

To set the scene for exploration of the two aspects to be highlighted, it is useful to pick up the threads of how they have so far been approached. As to the first, work describing what young children make of the written word, and how they set about reading, seems most relevant. This is not extensive and consists mainly of descriptions of pre-school success and of the attitudes and understandings of children in infant school classes. It is surprising that so little research has centred on what children actually do, rather than on how they should be taught. Presumably this reflects an assumption that reading skill cannot be drawn out or discovered, but must be the outcome of some kind of training or implanting when the passive recipient is ready. An assumption of active exploration and mastery on the part of the learner would surely have tipped the balance the other way, and what research we have on children's approaches to reading suggests that this might be the more appropriate assumption to make.

From such research it can be very firmly concluded that the early success stories reveal a very active interest and 'pressing to know' on the part of the child. Such motivation often implies a growing understanding that written words 'say something' and that people can say what they 'say'. In the course of an article describing learning in a very young child indeed, Krippner (1963) referred to Durkin's (1961, 1962) studies of pre-school readers in which she concluded that success came not from parental pressure but from a response to a 'word-filled world', and to repeated questioning of adults and siblings about it.

This urge to discovery and to active exploration was also mentioned by Clark (1976) in her study of young fluent readers. Although she was investigating the abilities of children who had entered school, she tried to relate these to their early reading and related experiences. She reported that many of the parents had felt embarrassed by their children's early success, because they felt that learning to read was a task to be achieved at school. Some had even attempted discouragement but found it impossible, and help had been given to the children not in order to develop their reading but to follow the children's interests. A strong sense of continued initiative by the children emerged from their own replies to the question of what they would do if they got stuck when reading. The most common answer was that they would ask their mother or father, but if both were too busy they would carry on by themselves. They might just go on to the next word to see if they could guess what the unknown word was, they might try to spell it out or sound it, or just miss it out. The suggestions of guessing or missing out clearly conveyed that the children were reading for meaning and doing the best they could with the text. Difficulties did not deter them.

But not all children find their parents hesitant about helping them to read. Soderbergh (1975) reported on the early reading of her own daughter. It is quite clear from the account that the child was actively engaged together with her mother in the process of learning to read. Her comments about their activities showed both interest and enthusiasm for exploration of what words can 'say'. Reading as an activity came to make some sort of sense. It may at first have meant little, or nothing more than a game with her mother, similar to some of the speech play she enjoyed, but, as it began to be genuine reading, the child realised something of the communicative intent behind writing.

This understanding of the writing act may come in very different ways and over varied periods of time for different children, and how it comes may be more to do with the way adults use print and writing in their daily lives, both with their children and in their hearing, than it has to do with deliberate attempts to foster reading skill. Vygotsky (1962) commented on the vague ideas of the usefulness of reading held by children beginning school; and Downing (1979) has taken some trouble to explore what is known of children's ideas in various countries and cultures, finding this vagueness to be widespread. This uncertainty and confusion has several aspects and it takes some effort to clarify them.

Some of the best reports of such effort are to be found in Reid's (1966) descriptions of children's replies to her questions about reading practices in their homes, and about what they thought about their own attempts to read. It was clear that children who had just started schooling often thought of pictures rather than text when asked what was in books, and there was confusion over ideas of words, letters and numbers. Equally vague were their ideas of the use of lettering in the world at large. Reid commented that the children had little idea of what the activity of reading would be like and what use or value it might have for them. Their understanding grew with experience during their sixth year. Another investigation (Francis, 1975) yielded similar findings. Although some children did come to school with some appreciation of the nature and functions of reading, others seemed to have very vague ideas even after a year or so of schooling. Further, there was a relationship between motivation and understanding. Those children with a growing appreciation of reading reported liking it, and anticipated with pleasure what they might read next, and even how they would read to their own children in the future. Those with vague understanding reported a range of rather different motivation from dislike, through tolerance, to trying in order to please a parent or teacher.

The aspect of vagueness in understanding that is to be emphasised here, and traced in this book, is that of not grasping that script is a medium of communication. Unlike learning to talk, when effective exchange about the important business of daily life is the prime motivator, and when reflection on the act of speaking is not called for, learning to read is frequently not motivated by a desire for effective communication, and conscious awareness that words may be used to influence actions or beliefs may be a necessary condition for success. This is what it means to know that words 'say something'. As far as words in speech are concerned, children begin to demonstrate this knowledge when they go beyond talking itself and comment on aspects of speech acts they have observed. When they also grasp that what is said can be recorded, as in memory or on tape, and can be thought about later, and then go on to identify writing as recorded words, they are in a position to understand the writing act. Considerable differences must exist between children in their experience of the implications of communication in the domestic culture, which itself reflects the social culture to which the parents belong. How much better placed for learning is the child on whom it has dawned that somehow the story or the information he wants can be discovered from the print that holds it, than is the child to whom the activity of reading is uncomprehended, not necessarily because no one reads to him but because he does not understand what is happening when they do. This is all a complex matter, but one far too easily taken for granted or ignored when considering children's learning to read. It takes a considerable effort of imagination for the literate adult to see script through the eyes of the non-reading child. A fascinating insight into a problem of understanding the kind of thing words 'say' is given by Soderbergh in her study. The child at 3 was being helped to compile her personal reading book, and insisted on the truth of what was written in her book. (An illness in her father prevented one sentence from coming true, and she then refused to allow it to stand.) How far, as in early speech, is truth value important in early reading? If one considers both the problem of the nature of the reality of words and that of the truth requirement, it is possible to begin to appreciate reasons why some children beginning to read in school 'stall' when faced with simple text. Fantasy and reality must both be accepted, and the realities of words must be approached with an exploratory attitude if text is to be acceptable. This is probably a more important issue than that of relevance to everyday life, though the latter is more often discussed.

Motivation and understanding, however, are not all in learning to read. Although the actual skill of deriving meaning from text may seem to come almost magically, its development takes some time. The young fluent reader who begins to read words and simple sentences at 3 or 4 has already gained much relevant skill, and still has some way to go to reach his fluency at 6 or 7. Soderbergh's study is particularly interesting in that what might be involved over a period of time is described in some detail, and it brings out the second feature highlighted in this book – grasp of orthography. Soderbergh began by showing her daughter a word printed on a card and telling her what it was. Each day words presented previously were checked for recognition before a new word was introduced.

For the first six weeks no day saw more than one new word, forty words were used, and all were either nouns or action verbs. The child obviously enjoyed the recognition game. After six weeks any new cards covered the vocabulary of a very short book, and by this time the child sometimes asked for more than one word per day. Judging by the child's behaviour, one of her learning problems at this time centred on words such as interrogatives, for which there was no easy way of strengthening the association with speech by indicating the object or action to which reference was being made. She was being required to use some such words at about the same time as she was first using them in speech. She did not, however, find the task impossible, especially when her mother wrote a specially devised book to suit her speech abilities, and introduced new 'function' words in simple sentence contexts rather than as isolated cards.

After three months she was able to read her first short book, and could recognise a total of 120 words. During this time she had also been told the 'names' of various letters, and some of her comments about them showed some learning of letter discrimination. Other comments drew attention to visual similarities between whole words. The overall characteristics of this introduction to reading could be said to be a carefully monitored 'look and say' approach, combined with an appreciation of the importance of the material being in some way meaningful to the child. The outcome of three months' steady work was a confident reading of words and sentences which were already familiar, both on sight and in speech. There was no evidence of ability to move beyond the familiar. Teachers will recognise this kind of progress among 5-year-old children in school, though it is doubtful whether the introduction of new words can be so finely graded and suited to individual learning with a class of anything up to thirty or so pupils.

During the next few weeks the child revealed more of what the reading meant to her. She enjoyed her books well enough to take them, look at them and comment on them quite spontaneously. Her first book became an interesting toy, providing a game she could play by herself or with her mother. She accepted new function words by suggesting sentences containing them to check their meaning or use, thus showing a growing awareness of individual words in speech. Moreover, she revealed an interesting conceptual problem in that she seemed to read a phrase such as *pushing a pram* not only as referring to the act of pushing a baby-carriage, but also as describing the act of pushing the card carrying the word *pram*. It was during the period of accumulation of new books, after about six months of learning to read, that the Soderbergh child began to read new words before being told what they were. Her first eleven attempts were carefully selected for her and she approached them very attentively. She was successful with nine. As she gained confidence and was willing to take more risks, her success rate fell, but her absolute mastery increased. It is usually claimed that a phonic approach is indicated for coping with words not previously met, but this child had no such instruction and made no attempts to 'sound' the letters she could identify by name. She often compared words on the basis of initial-letter similarity, and sometimes through other common letters or letter patterns.

Soderbergh analysed the first correct new readings and inferred strategies of recognising elements previously encountered in familiar words, and their combinations or deletions in the new. Thus, to invent English examples, *pushchair* might be recognised from *push* and *chair*, and, although bound morpheme recognition came fractionally later, *cooked* might be seen as *cook* and *ed*. Similarly *cook* might have been read through a deletion strategy if *cooked* and *ed* were familiar. Further analysis of success and of misreadings revealed an increasing grasp of the orthography of Swedish and of the ability to recognise quite complex patterns of letters. This involved length of word, order of lettering and grouping of letters. What is fascinating is the way this ability was linked with the ability to read new words aloud without an explicit phonic approach. Whatever links were made between the sight and sound of words in the child's mental store were unconscious and entirely adequate. After a year of steady learning the child could read any new word given to her in the book building game; and she could initiate games such as 'What am I thinking of? It begins with ——' and the letter was named, not sounded, while the intended solution was apt.

One further observation in this delightfully detailed study shows how the individually presented words were not simply listed in the mental store, or stored only on a basis of graphic patterning, but were also remembered in meaningful contexts. The child on one occasion was observed sorting the word cards into three piles. At that time she had read three short books; and, as she sorted, she rehearsed sentences in which the word was found, and her resulting three piles represented the vocabularies of each book.

A study by MacKinnon (1959) of the reading attempts of children in their first year at school, using the Gibson–Richards reading materials, revealed similar strategies to those of the Soderbergh child. Again the presentation of new words was controlled but not as tightly as in the Soderbergh approach, and children made letter discriminations well before they had amassed a 'base' of a hundred words or so. Nevertheless a strong reliance on familiar, already learned, words and sentences was shown, as were successes and misreadings suggesting recognition of letter patterns. Again no 'phonic' approach was attempted or explicitly developed, but signs of breaking into new presentations were evident. That children tend to use such strategies with even less tightly controlled presentation was shown in another study (Francis, 1977) of children beginning to read in two very different schools with different approaches to presenting the same reading material.

There is evidence, then, of children learning a good deal about spelling in their language (and at a more complex level than simple ordering of letters) before they are able to 'spell' many words correctly, and before they explicitly attempt letter–sound correspondences. It appears to be incidental learning, acquired through experience of looking at and identifying members of a set of words which are compared with each other. In the cases outlined here it seemed to be sufficient to lead children into a position of being able to read new words, and to read fluently, without any overt attempts at using 'phonics' of any kind. This suggests that, at least for some children, explicit phonics is unnecessary, and that for others it may be a more cumbersome way of learning than a more visual approach. Questions that remain must be how the covert linking of sight and sound takes place when it is not overtly attempted at any finer level of analysis than the word, whether there are pupils for whom a phonics method *must* be used, and how pupils respond to phonics teaching at different stages of 'spelling awareness'.

No attempt is made in this book to answer the first question; the second will be discussed in the light of the study; while the third will be explored as one of its central concerns.

The rest of this book is a report of a study of early reading in school, carried out in the light of the issues raised in this introductory chapter. For most of their first three years of schooling ten children were seen almost weekly, and their progress was explored in a variety of ways. It was also set against that of other children in the same school and compared with that of children in a school in a very different catchment area. One of the problems of observing for such a long period was the possibility that the sample children might benefit from the attention they received, while another was the difficulty of refraining from specifically trying to help them. The former was dealt with by giving sufficient attention to the other children to mask the sampling effect, and the latter by exercising considerable self-restraint.

Chapter 2

Developing a Study

A RESEARCH STRATEGY

Given that understanding the acts of writing and reading and
knowing something of the spelling system were the two features of
early reading to be examined, it was necessary to plan a research
strategy which might allow this without distorting the children's
learning. The objectives did not indicate an experimental design,
for no comparisons were to be made, but they did suggest that case
studies might be appropriate, and that observation over the first
years of schooling might be necessary. This would enable the
phenomena to be studied in the context of other aspects of learning
to read, and provide some preliminary idea of their relative importance. Clearly, observation studies of this kind required intensive
exploration of each child, and a single observer could only study a
limited number of children. Techniques of exploration would include talking with the children, structured interviews with them,
and recording behaviours most relevant to their reading and writing. To help interpret the studies it would be necessary to formally
assess their abilities and to describe the contexts of learning –
materials and methods in home, school and classroom. It was
decided to limit the number of children to ten and to work with a
sample of five boys and five girls. In order to catch a sample who had
made little progress by the time they entered school and who,
nevertheless, might prove to learn at different rates and in different
ways, a random sample was chosen from the intake of a school in a
somewhat disadvantaged area of a large city.

SELECTING THE CHILDREN

A school was selected on advice from the local education authority.
It served a housing estate where there was a tradition of manual
employment, especially in transport services for men and cleaning
and tailoring for women. In periods of high unemployment it was a
vulnerable area, and even in good times some families lived in
poverty. The school provided for children from 4 to 9 years of age,

all entering during their fifth year. The full intake of eighty-eight in the year prior to the study had been investigated by an educational psychologist at the request of the headteacher, in order to provide information for school policy decisions. This meant that general information was available about abilities on starting school. At an average age of 4 years 10 months measures of the children's general intellectual ability yielded a mean score well below the norm for their age. 'Reading readiness' scores on vocabulary and concept development were also below average, while on auditory and visual discrimination tests many children failed to cope with the task. Their copying skills were also poor. On personal and social development scales the children did better. They could generally look after themselves and play with others as well as most children of their age; their speech development was only marginally retarded; and they were able to give basic information about themselves. This discrepancy between educational and personal/social development was not surprising in an area where 60 per cent of the children were found to rate at least one of the indices of social disadvantage used by the National Children's Bureau in its national study. Two indices were particularly notable. Single-parent families were the experience of 20 per cent of the children (national figure 6 per cent), while 52 per cent received free school meals (national figure 14 per cent). It was noticeable that the children looked immature, and in fact they were found to be very definitely shorter and lighter than would be expected for their age.

When the staff of the school were approached to discuss a possible study of children's learning to read, the class teacher of those children in the first year whose birthdays fell between January and April was particularly interested. It was therefore decided to draw a sample from her class. Five boys and five girls were selected by drawing names from a hat. Fortunately not one of these left the school until the third year, so it was possible to trace their learning for some time.

THEIR ABILITIES AND SKILLS

An overall picture of the abilities of the ten was needed to provide a useful framework for the rest of the study. To this end it was decided to use a selection of tests of general ability and of reading abilities for which norms were available, and to supplement these with some assessment of writing and oral language skills. The reader is advised at this point to acquaint himself with the programme outlined on p. 17 and given fully in the Appendices. Reference will frequently be made to various tests. Test scores for those which could be meaningfully compared, in terms of either norms or rank-ordering, are shown in Table 2.1.

As a first task in early January in the first year all ten children were asked, individually, but within the classroom and as part of their general activities, to copy carefully the figures shown in the Appendix, Test A1. They used their own school pencils, and sheets of paper were supplied to match the size of the sample sheet. Each sheet was placed squarely on the table in front of the child and the sample sheet was placed beyond it so that neither hand obscured the view during copying. A scoring system was devised, based on features of break and position of break in circular figures, and vertical, horizontal and slanting orientation in straight-line figures. The scoring is shown with the figures in the Appendix, Test A1. The children's total scores are given in Table 2.1.

All the children attempted the task seriously and all copied the first three figures acceptably; some managed more, and one child was able to reproduce all but the diamond in a firm, well-arranged manner. The three major difficulties were the complexity of figures of more than one line, the orientation of the slanting straight lines, and the position of the gaps in curved figures. It was concluded that before the children could be expected to copy letters accurately they would need practice in identifying important distinctive features and in controlling their pencil movements to match them. Their baseline skill was, however, sufficient to justify the attempts made by the teacher to guide the children through tracing and copying tasks.

After copying the figures the children were given fresh sheets of paper and asked to draw a man, the best picture of a man that they could draw. It was necessary to define *man* as *mister* (the local dialect equivalent) to ensure comprehension of the task. The children were given all the time they needed until they indicated they were satisfied with their pictures, and they appeared to enjoy the task. As in the copying task, they showed sufficient motor dexterity to produce recognisable features. For one or two children one wondered at first sight whether the task was too much for them in this respect; but, judging by their figure copying, it seemed that the difficulty lay in deciding what to draw rather than in perceptual-motor control. The drawings ranged from a disjointed and very simple figure, similar to the typical drawing of younger children, to a sketch complete with body, head, facial detail, hair, ears, neck, limbs, feet, hands, fingers and some indication of good proportion and of clothing. The task was scored as for the Goodenough Draw-a-Man test (Harris, 1963). It was repeated three months later, when a very similar ranking was obtained, as shown by

Table 2.1 *Children's Test Scores*

	FIRST YEAR (1975–6)				SECOND YEAR (1976–7)				THIRD YEAR (1977–8)			
	Figure copying* (max. 26) (Jan.)	Draw-a-Man (March)	Break through* reading (max. 30) (April)	Break through* reading (June)	Figure copying* (Oct.)	Break through* reading (Nov.)	Daniels and Diack (May)	Schonell A (June)	EPVT (Oct.)	Daniels and Diack (Feb.)	Schonell A (June)	Chron. Age (June)
JOHN	23	102	19	29	25	30	8:3	7:9	122	9:0	11:0	7:2
WILMA	20	110	21	24	25	25	6:2	6:1	105	7:3	7:6	7:3
MARY	17	104	9	17	22	20	5:8	5:8	110	–	–	7:3
SEAN	23	92	6	16	26	14	5:8	5:7	111	6:6	6:9	7:3
DAVE	9	92	4	5	19	8	5:2	5:2	106	5:9	6:6	7:3
MATT	9	84	0	0	18	0	no score	5:2	98	5:6	6:7	7:2
AMANDA	14	100	0	0	22	0	no score	no score	–	–	–	7:3
MICHAEL	16	80	1	0	16	0	no score	no score	87	no score	5:9	7:2
SARA	12	84	0	0	15	0	no score	no score	–	–	–	7:6
FIONA	11	84	0	0	11	0	no score	no score	78	–	–	7:4

* Raw scores on non-standardised test. Other tests give standardised scores (mean 100), or reading ages.

the standardized conversion of the average raw scores in Table 2.1.

In order to estimate the usefulness of these tests as predictors of later reading ability at the end of the school year, rank-order correlations between Draw-a-Man, copying and reading were calculated. Both the drawing scores predicted quite well, but a composite ranking, combining Draw-a-Man with figure copying ranks, gave a higher correlation with reading than did either alone. It would seem that both skills contributed to learning to read, one perhaps because it involved symbolic representation, and the other because it drew on pattern discrimination and reproduction. Comparison of the Draw-a-Man scores with the norms for the Goodenough scale suggested that on average both girls and boys scored below the norms for their age-group. As regards chronological age they fell at the boundary between the two Goodenough categories of 4–5 and 5–6 years respectively. The best estimate of the girls' average standard score was about 95 and that of the boys' was 90. These compare with a mean of 100 on a scale with a standard deviation of 15. It could be reasonably suggested, then, that in so far as the Goodenough scale measures intellectual maturity the children were below the average for their age.

At the end of this second term, in April, the children were given the informal reading test shown in the Appendix, Test A5. The first part comprised a list of thirty words from those in the Breakthrough scheme which the teacher had chosen to present first. Words which were recognised by none of the children were *like, home, good, baby, he, birthday* and *are. Dog, school* and *my* were each recognised by one child, and *boy, the, house, can, girl, at, in, we, it, on* and *bed* by two. *Television* and *cat* were recognised by three children, *a, big, little, am* and *see* by four and *I* by five. This distribution may well have reflected the children's experience with a few simple sentences such as *I am a boy (or girl), I see (or like) television* and *I see (or like) my cat.* On this view it was surprising that *like* was not recognised.

The second part of the test presented eight simple sentences from those typically used in classwork, using eight words which were in the first part of the test and also the plural *dogs.* Fiona and Sara could read nothing in either part of the test, while Michael read *I* only in both; but for the other children it was interesting to find that the different contexts influenced the words read. Dave, for instance, was able to read *see* and *dog* in the sentences in addition to the words he read in the test. On the other hand he misread *my* (which he had not read in the list) giving *am* (which he had correctly read in the list). Such errors led one to wonder how correct a correct reading really was. Perhaps Dave associated *on* in a two-letter word with *am*, rather than relating the word to the total visual representation. He also read sentences by giving a sensible completion if he could get as far as the verb (or if the verb was supplied); but he did so within the context of the Breakthrough vocabulary, possibly switching to a sentence or part of a sentence he had previously encountered in classwork. Another interesting point was that while he correctly read *dog* and *television* after *I see a*, he failed to read them with an unrecognised verb context. Sean and Mary showed similar differences in success with particular words in different contexts, failing to read words in the list which were later read in sentences, and showing graphic (letter-based) confusion errors such as *little* for *television*, *red* for *are* and *cat* for *can*. They did not, however, show the same verb-object specificity. They could read the same object noun independently of verb variation. This is presumably part of more knowledgeable reading. John and Wilma read all the sentence words correctly except for *like*, even reading the *dog/dogs* difference correctly. Their errors showed in list reading, where some confusions occurred, as in *home* with *house* and *big* with *dog*. These suggested awareness of spelling patterns in words in English.

The first part of the Breakthrough test was repeated towards the end of the third term after an interval of two months. Scores improved for those children who had had any success the first time; the others, however, made marginal or no progress. There was virtually no evidence of forgetting previously known words, and clearly all the children were still learning, or attempting to learn, these early words in their scheme.

At the beginning of the children's second compulsory school year (during which they reached the age of 6) they were given an extended version of the copying test A1, (Appendix A) used in the previous year. This new form (B1, Appendix B) allowed comparison with earlier copying of the first eleven items, but introduced four items which were unambiguously letters of the alphabet. This time the lay-out of the figures was copied much more accurately by all the children, the use of rows and columns being particularly clearer in the case of the less able copiers. Complexity no longer posed a problem with these particular patterns, but orientation of diagonals and of gaps in closure still presented difficulty for some. In general the pencil was used more firmly and confidently in reproducing line. There was no difference in handedness between the two testings for any of the children.

There were interesting differences in copying the different kinds of item. Two children, Mary and Sean, copied the letters and the geometric figures with equal care, firmness and attention to proportion; but the others copied the letters with less neat lay-out, greater wobble in line and more variation in size than for the geometric figures. The explanation seemed to lie either in a different level of attention to the copying (as if, for instance, the letters carried greater meaning or led to more anxiety) or in some greater difficulty in combining straight lines with curves. Six of the children copied the letters correctly, in spite of their untidy appearance; but both Michael and Matt reversed the *d* to give *b*, while Sara produced four *p*s instead of *d*, *p*, *b* and *g*, and Fiona drew four very wobbly shapes with poor closure and no ascending vertical lines. All four had trouble with the diagonal orientations in the geometrical forms, and Fiona also had problems with closure. There was thus some correspondence between copying of the two kinds of figures in so far as reproduction of essential features was used.

Since the children had been asked to write their first names on their papers, it was possible to compare their free letter writing with their copying. The same untidy, uneven formation was evident, but Wilma, Mary, John, Dave and Sean all produced correctly spelled versions with no orientation or reversal errors. Amanda's only error was a reversed *n*. The other four children were unable to write their names, though Fiona did make an attempt. She produced a string of ten shapes, of which only three letters were recognisable. Michael and Sara were willing to try to copy their names, Sara making only one error with a reversed *a*, and Michael producing a complete name reversal by writing from right to left but making no letter reversals. Matt, however, was unwilling to try to write or to copy his name. The overall pattern, then, was that the children's copying abilities had improved over the previous nine months, but that the ability to copy letters was less secure than that of reproducing simple geometric patterns, and that the production of their own first names (the free writing task most likely to be done successfully) was not possible for four of the ten children.

In November, since all the children were still working with the Breakthrough scheme, Test A5 (Appendix A) was tried again. This time John read entirely successfully, while Wilma and Mary did very well. New learning had not interfered with the old, but Sean and Dave had hardly improved at all, while the other five children could still not read a single word.

No further test was tried with the children until they were given the Daniels and Diack (1958) reading test as a routine measure in the school in May. It was thought that the Schonell Graded Word Recognition test (Schonell, 1945) might examine a rather different aspect of reading skill, and this was given in June. A considerable measure of agreement was found, and, not surprisingly in the light of other observations, only five of the children managed to score and so register a 'reading age'. By now Sara had left the school, and Fiona, Michael and Amanda failed to score on either test. Scores for the others are shown in Table 2.1, from which, given that the corresponding chronological ages were all about 6 years, it can be seen that, apart from Wilma and John, reading ability was well below the norm.

In the third school year, when the children were approaching their seventh birthdays, it was felt that further standardised tests could be used to assess their abilities and diagnose difficulties. Accordingly, much of the time spent with them in their third year in school was used for such testing, not only of the original sample, but of all the children in their class. At this stage Amanda had moved to another school.

The English Picture Vocabulary test (Brimer and Dunn, 1962) was used as a measure of verbal ability. Testing of the sample children was begun in October and that of the whole class was completed in February. The standardised scores for the whole class, including Fiona, yielded a mean of 101·5 with a standard deviation of 9·5, and a range of 78–125. The mean was perhaps rather high for a class of socially disadvantaged children, but it should be remembered that the tester was very familiar to the children and the testing situation was easy and friendly. The standard deviation was low (that for the test standardisation sample was 15), there being a very close bunching about the mean. This was not surprising in a socially disadvantaged group of children, who largely found familiar objects and situations easy to name, but who found some objects unfamiliar, and abstract words hard to identify. The usefulness of the original sample, which was chosen on a random basis, can be estimated from their mean of 102·1 (n = 8) and standard deviation of 13·2. Rather than reflecting the bunching it covered the spread. The rank-ordering of scores was surprising only in that Wilma's score was lower than might have been predicted from her reading and classwork. The order ran – John, Sean, Mary, Dave, Wilma, Matt, Michael and Fiona.

By February only six of the ten children in the original sample remained in the school, for by now both Fiona and Mary had also left. These six were given the Daniels and Diack Standard Reading test, while the headteachers of the schools to which the other children had moved were approached for information about their progress. Of the six remaining children, Michael achieved no score, Dave and Matt managed a few items and obtained reading ages between 5 and 6 years, while Sean, Wilma and John did better, Wilma scoring at the norm and John reaching the 9-year ceiling for the test. Of the children who had changed schools, Mary was said to be reading adequately for her general schoolwork, but no reading test had been given, while Amanda, at 7 years 6 months, and Sara, at 7 years 9 months, had both been assessed at a reading age of 6 years 7 months on a different test (Young, 1968). Apart from a second testing with the Schonell test, this was the last standardised or useful rank-yielding test to be used.

Table 2.1 has three major features. Most of the children performed at or below the norm, the rank-ordering of children was very similar across tests, and the reading scores lagged behind the general cognitive measures. Undoubtedly a sample of children had been selected whose learning to read was slow, but among whom some were learning successfully.

How the standardised tests were fitted into the total research programme can be seen from Table 2.2. Certain tasks in this total array were set because language development has frequently been cited as having a direct bearing on learning to read, and it was felt that this factor ought to be examined if a proper assessment of the main factors of interest was to be made.

LANGUAGE AND READING

A first consideration was whether the children's command of language was sufficient to support their reading. Soderbergh's child was initially speaking in the somewhat 'telegraphic' style characteristic of the 2–3-year-old, but, although it suggested a need for special attention to understanding the functions of sentence 'frame' words, this did not prevent learning. Yet many suggestions are to be found in the literature on reading to the effect that socially disadvantaged children have a language deficit or difference that is retarding in its effect on school learning. The important research problem seemed to be to judge the adequacy of the children's speech in the various tasks they might meet in school, especially those highly relevant to learning to read.

The first task attempted was to examine the children's ability to give some oral account which might be similar in structure to a simple written text, that is, anything from a simple sentence to a paragraph. Some reference to a state of affairs was required, and the first task was simply to talk about a picture or two in a picture-book from the classroom bookstand.

Within the first month of the study the children were quite willing to leave the classroom one by one with the observer, and to sit at a small table in the corridor nearby to look at a picture-book from the class supply. The conversation between observer and child was recorded and no child seemed to mind this procedure. In the case of

Table 2.2: *Programme of Reported Testing of Reading and Language Skills*

TERM	YEAR 1 Age 4½–5½	YEAR 2 Age 5½–6½	YEAR 3 Age 6½–7½
AUTUMN		Figure copying (B1) Visual discrimination/reading tests (B2) Breakthrough test (A5) Classwork samples of reading and writing Story recall (B3) Sample of reading	EPVT Sample of reading Orthographic knowledge tests (C1–3)
SPRING	Figure copying (A1) Draw-a-Man test Speech sampling Letter/number discrimination (A2) Letters/words/sentences (A3) Reading interview Reading schedule (A4) Breakthrough reading test (A5)	Story recall (B4) Use of language tests (B5) Sample of reading	Sample of reading EPVT for whole class Reading interview Daniels and Diack Standard and Diagnostic tests
SUMMER	Draw-a-Man test Sample of reading Breakthrough test (A5) Sample of reading	Sample of writing Sample of reading Interviews with parents Sample of reading Reading schedule (B7) Daniels, Diack Standard test Schonell Graded Word Recognition test (A)	Sample of reading Teachers' reports Schonell (A)

one or two children who virtually refrained from talking the re-
corder was packed away, but this did not lead them to be any more
forthcoming. Indeed, the same children at that stage often refused
to speak with the teacher in the ordinary run of classroom activities.
The book contained some pictures of isolated objects and others of
scenes, while a few were series depicting simple stories. The children were encouraged to comment on all three kinds, but left free to
make their own choice. The aims were to explore understanding
and interpretation of picture material, and to sample speech in that
context. If a child spoke of other things, however, this was not
discouraged since any speech was regarded as useful. The transcrip-
tions of the recorded speech were used to identify various aspects of
understanding and speech, emphasis lying on any skills or difficulties the children revealed.

There was considerable variety in the manner of talking: Wilma,
John, Sean and Michael were active partners while Dave was
relatively passive. Mary, Amanda and Fiona were rather diffident
and shy while Matt was so retiring that attempts at conversation
seemed really painful. He, in fact, said nothing! Articulation revealed clear dialect features, but in addition to these the children,
like many 5-year-olds, tended to have difficulty pronouncing *r* and
tl. Thus *carrot* was pronounced more like *cawwot* and *bottle* like
bokkle. Wilma, Sara, John and Dave spoke most clearly, while Sean
was a little less clear; Fiona was quite hard to hear and Michael had
such articulation problems that he had been referred to a speech
therapist for help. One of his main difficulties was an almost
invariable dropping of final consonants.

Sentence length and complexity varied considerably, depending
at least in part on the structure of the conversation. One-word
answers, and even one-word spontaneous comments, were frequently used when referring to pictures of single objects; while the
answers to questions and the comments about scenes tended to take
predicate forms such as *falling over backwards*, thus omitting
reference to the subject. Sequences of comments, sometimes in
complex sentences, tended to be related to series of pictures inviting
a story. Wilma, John and Sean were the only three who did produce
such sequences. Constructions of interest included the use of infini-
tive clauses, clauses introduced by *because*, and conjunctions in
both subject and predicate phrases. Two of the complex sentences
produced were *That's a little girl helping mam because she's getting a
baby* (Wilma) and *A boy and his dad are going to the hospital to visit
the mam* (John). Sometimes it was doubtful whether the children
fully understood constructions they were using; but they did introduce comparative phrases like *smaller than,* and they used adjec-

tives to qualify nouns. They did not always name colours correctly, and showed a tendency to list items, or count them, rather than create an idea around them. One might have hazarded a guess that if symbolic representation in pictures might relate to that in print, then most of the children might take up single-word recognition, but possibly only Wilma, John and Sean would readily take up reading with meaning. (Mary was absent for this interview.) But the restriction was less to do with command of sentence production, for all who spoke at all spoke well enough at the simple sentence level, and more to do with difficulty in formulating an idea to talk about.

Since only Wilma, John and Mary made early progress with reading which required them to cope with more than single sentences, a further exploration was not undertaken until the following November, in the second year of schooling. It was thought at this stage that some sampling of the children's spoken language related to story-telling might be useful, since reading and writing was soon to require remembering and anticipating meaning over a passage of story rather than within a single sentence. A story (Test B3, Appendix B) was selected from a story-book in use in the classroom, being one not yet heard by the children, and was read individually to each child who was then asked to retell it in his own way. Each child was forewarned of the expected retelling. The children enjoyed being read to individually, and also seemed to enjoy the story. The retelling produced the interesting finding that some of the children settled for a very brief summary and others for a single comment, though further prompting revealed that they could recall much more. It seemed fair to conclude that comprehension was adequate, that the retelling was adequate if it was accepted in a question and answer form, but that a story form was either alien or too difficult. Thus any handicap relating to story reading that may have been detected seemed not to lie in spoken language *per se*, but in expressing a coherent set of ideas in a narrative form.

As to questions of articulation and dialect affecting the task, it was clear that dialect was the order of the day in retelling, but that no child seemed hampered in comprehension by differences between the rendering in Standard English and his own dialect. There was some evidence of articulation immaturity, but Michael's particular speech handicap was less evident than formerly. Any question of how dialect might affect reading was seen to be a complex problem when it was realised that at least two levels, the phonetic and the lexical, had to be considered, and that on both counts the children's use of the Standard English form was context-dependent within their dialect. The analysis of several accounts, some mentioned later in the book, makes this very clear.

It seemed fairly certain at this stage that any failure in communication by the child, which might retard his learning to read, was less likely to lie in difficulty in formulating or responding to speech than in problems of not communicating enough with the teacher or of not understanding the teacher's terminology or purpose. Language could not be separated from intentions and ideas. After the Christmas holiday it was decided to explore the children's speech and cognitive skills with an eye to the question of how each might bear on the other.

The first task was repetition of a story used previously by the author in other schools (Francis, 1975), and printed in Appendix B as Test B4. Even allowing for the time interval since the 'Kangaroo and Joey' story before Christmas, this second story seemed more useful in eliciting more speech and more of a story sequence in the children's retelling, though only marginally so for Matt. It was not, then, the case that the children could not express a story idea, but that the story tasks differed in their power to release such expression, either because of content differences or because of some task familiarity effect. The children's accounts could be scored for length (number of words) and story cohesion (grading from impression), and when this was done the two story tasks yielded high rank-order correlations between both the number of words and the story cohesion ratings. Length also correlated with cohesion. Both measures correlated positively and well with reading ability, but no direction could reasonably be attributed to the relationships – indeed, it was likely that both literacy and oral story grasp were feeding each other, and together adding momentum to all-round achievement in school. The cohesion of the stories was related to the complexity of sentence structure in the children's accounts. Mary, in particular, produced a selection of connectives including *because, if, who* and *after*. One interesting point about the retelling was the occasional occurrence, without exact imitation, of more formal grammatical expression than seemed characteristic of the children's conversational speech, even to a teacher. Perhaps they had learned that story-telling had a formal or ritual aspect to it, and this would not be surprising in view of the nature of their classroom experience of listening to the teacher reading. Obviously the children's everyday speech style or register did not prevent their adopting new ways, though children from homes where more formal register or style was more frequently encountered might be at a relative advantage.

Story relating is only one of the language uses expected of children in primary schools and related to reading. They are also expected to understand and produce explanations, hypothetical consequences and comparisons of quality and quantity, often in relation to an ongoing practical task, but also in verbal exchange and in reading and written work. It was with a view to assessing the ten children's abilities to cope with aspects of these uses that a group of exploratory tests was devised.

The first, Appendix B, Test B5(1), was to try to elicit verbal explanation in a simple individual questioning about the nature of snow. The subject was selected because of its topicality and mystery. There had just been quite a substantial snowfall – the first real fall for two or three years and therefore a matter exciting considerable astonishment and curiosity. Similar questions were addressed to each child, but the structure of the interview was a developing interaction. The first, and most obvious, observation was that the children did not need to give cast-iron and grammatically complete explanations. It would have seemed very odd and unnatural to have done so in a conversational situation. What was quite clear was that some oddly formed remarks carried what was taken to be an appropriate intended meaning. Any gap between expression and understanding was not simply a matter of choice of expression. When Amanda replied to *What makes the snow melt?* with *'Cos rain*, and the rain had in fact disposed of the snow, it seemed sensible to conclude that this explanation went as far as covering what was associated with the melting without actually saying anything about the process. But an answer of the form *It melted because it rained* would have been no more useful as an explanation in spite of its more formal nature. Amanda's answer to the next question *How does the rain make it melt?* was *It water it.* There was still no reference to temperature or to heat transfer, which the concept of melting entailed, but there was, in spite of the grammatical form of the answer, sufficient to suggest that Amanda was thinking of a change of state. *It changes it to water* would have been more explicit but not more informative of the child's understanding.

Some positive points could be made about the children's understanding as far as they seemed able to express it. They brought out a variety of causes for the melting and, due to the actual weather conditions during the period of snow, it was possible to differentiate between a popular wisdom attributing melting to sunshine, and observation of factors actually associated with the melting, such as rain, wind, fog, cloud, salt and standing on the snow. Some children included both popular and observed associations. As to the processes of melting and freezing, a few children managed to convey that the factors mentioned were involved in a process of change of state, and that heat and cold figured in it, but the crucial point of heat transfer or of temperature difference was not made, as, indeed, one could scarcely expect it to be at this age. Others, however, failed to give a reasonably clear association of circumstances, but seemed to have sufficient use of language to have done so, while in some instances it was not clear whether the lack was of ideas or expression. Thus the quality of the verbal exchange varied from remarks on both sides that seemed to dovetail with mutual comprehension (whatever the level of the child's understanding of snow), to exchange where, in the cases of Fiona and Sara, half of the child's remarks seemed in no way to follow from the preceding adult remark, but rather to be loosely associated, random comment. In general the children all showed signs of command of the language forms needed to attempt explanation, but either failed to pin down conceptual aspects of the problem or failed to attempt to explain. It was interesting to see how quite odd or incomplete linguistic expression could yet be used to get something of an understanding across to the hearer.

Further exploration of language abilities which might be relevant to classroom tasks involving reading or writing was made using the tasks under B5–B7 in the Appendix. Essentially they were to examine use of such terms as *because, same, more, I think, it could be* and *it might be*, which have all been highlighted in the literature as presenting certain conceptual problems for children of this age (Piaget, 1928; Donaldson, 1978). It would distract from the main theme of this book to go into much detail on this point, but all the children showed some degree of familiarity with the expressions, and comprehended their use to some extent – the abler discriminating between different usage much as reported in the literature. Differences between the children in the range of their own use of the expressions were more marked, but again all demonstrated their use in some way or other. The main differences were not of availability of the forms of language in appropriate contexts, but of identifying and attending to relevant detail in the tasks concerned.

The general conclusion about the relationship between language abilities and learning to read was that no child would have been prevented from learning on the grounds of inadequate language development, but that some might be relatively slow for the following reasons. Unwillingness to talk with the teacher reduced learning opportunities. Insufficient 'negotiation' led to failure to identify relevant (in the adult's view) aspects of a learning task and so to incomprehension. Misapplication of certain terms could lead to misunderstanding of number tasks, which were also seen as part of learning to read and write. Not all the children were able to cope with narrative structure, even in heard stories, and most found its expression beyond them, yet much of their 'text' for learning to read and write was reporting and narrative. This implied assumptions that the children understood a particular purpose of writing among others, and that they had a certain mental processing maturity. Neither assumption could be made with confidence about the children in this study, so evaluation of their reading had to be made in this light.

THE MAIN OBJECTIVES

Since children's understanding of the act of writing and their learning about the spelling system were the main foci of interest, ways of exploring these were needed which went beyond evidence gleaned from the tests reported so far. It was necessary to consider how teaching in school and experience at home might affect these. So teachers were invited to explain their methods, reading schemes were examined and classroom activities were monitored, while mothers and children were interviewed about reading outside school. Children's ways of coping with text and with writing were explored by recording and analysing their performance. Chapter 3 will provide an account of the school experience of the children, and the following chapters will pursue the main questions.

Chapter 3

Reading in the Classroom

In order to appreciate the context of learning for the children, and so to be able to interpret test results and individual performance sensibly, regular visits were made to the classrooms. From time to time fairly lengthy periods of activity were sampled and the following pages provide the reader with an informal account of reading and writing in the classrooms, preceded by a description of the school's approach to teaching reading.

THE APPROACH TO READING

The school's general policy was to introduce the children to reading through a variety of pre-reading 'experiences', an induction into the *Breakthrough to Literacy* (Mackay *et al.*, 1970) activities, and a translation to the Gay Way reading scheme (Boyce, 1949).

Pre-reading activities included drawing, pattern copying and construction, left–right linear pattern drawing with letter-like and letter shapes, story-telling and construction, relating daily experiences, describing objects and labelling objects and personal property in the classroom. In all these the teacher acted as model and guide, and it was clear that for many of the children the activities were novel and not easy. Comparison with children in other schools led to an awareness of the slowness of these children's engagement in, and execution of, the tasks concerned. Enjoyment was generally evident but skill and speed were not.

The philosophy behind the Breakthrough approach is that reading and writing are complementary aspects of literacy and should be fostered together. The initial stages focus on sentence construction, while word building and analysis follow later. In principle, the teacher could devise his own materials to follow through the steps of the Breakthrough approach, but the devisers of the scheme have produced a ready-made set. The most important item is the sentence-maker, a three-sheet folder containing individual word cards together with a slotted stand in which these cards may be placed to form a sentence. Each card has a baseline to ensure it is placed the right way up, and habits of left to right placing and word spacing can be established. Each child has a personal folder, two sheets of which contain the basic stock of word cards given in the scheme, each card in a containing labelled pocket so that word matching is encouraged when putting the cards away. On the third sheet blank envelopes are ready to hold any additional words the child wishes to use in his sentence building. The teacher uses a large wall-hung replica of the two basic sheets of the folder, together with a large stand for group teaching activities. There are about 120 words to the basic store, with a few additional cards carrying suffixes such as *ing* and *s* to give grammatical flexibility when children can cope with the idea of using them. The teacher is free to create new word cards rather than using suffix cards if the children wish to use words like *reading* rather than *read* or *books* rather than *book*. Obviously a wish to use *making* rather than *make* would entail the provision of a new card or special attention at some point to the difference between *makeing* and *making*. When the child knows a small stock of words and has the idea of building a few sentences, he is able to work with his personal folder. Writing is learned by copying the constructed sentences, and writing from memory can be encouraged when this skill is established.

Observation in the school showed that the teachers were using the Breakthrough materials and following the principles of the scheme very carefully. Some children were making progress in the manner suggested by the Breakthrough manual, but a major problem was that many of the children were not responding as the manual led one to expect. For these children much more pre-reading activity was provided, and the initiation into the Breakthrough materials was prolonged and carried through very carefully. For those children who were making progress, and could construct a few small sentences of their own, the teacher began to provide additional words from the Gay Way basic reading scheme so that the idea of sentence construction could be carried forward as preparation for the first book in that scheme. As well as introducing the appropriate vocabulary, the teachers prepared accompanying pictures so that the children would recognise the context in which they could use these new words when the time came. The children who were making progress with reading were thus able to begin to read from the Gay Way scheme towards the end of their first year in school. This did not mean, however, that they ceased to use the Breakthrough approach. They continued to use their folder, adding new words as they invented new sentences, improving their sentence copying and moving towards free writing. This, however, was still at the single-sentence level. There were possibly two reasons for this with the children concerned. The habits of single-sentence construction may well have operated against an inclination to go further, but it also seemed true that the children lacked an initial wish or capacity to invent beyond the single sentence. Even after two years in this school many children who were reading reasonably well were not able to construct short stories or accounts of events in their daily lives. In other schools children were observed writing much more freely and readily even in their first year at school. Jessie Reid's (1966) evaluation of the *Breakthrough to Literacy* approach would also lead one to expect that children might write more readily when using these materials.

Lest it be thought that the approach to reading was solely through the sentence construction work, it should be made clear that word analysis and construction were attempted with most of the children during their first year in school. The teacher introduced this kind of work in group sessions and followed it up in individual work with children. It was clear that while many of the children were able to partake in the group activities, they were not able to transfer what they were learning to their own independent attempts to read and write. Observation of their reading and writing suggested that they were not able to use what is basically a more phonic approach until they had made considerable moves forward in their mastery of recognition reading. Improvement in word construction skills, however, did not necessarily lead to more or freer writing. With a few exceptions the children still seemed constrained in some way.

The designers of the Gay Way series of basic readers claim that it lends itself to sentence, whole-word and phonic approaches, and depends on a steady build-up of reading vocabulary with frequent repetition to aid learning. This being so, it would not seem to be unreasonable to link it with a Breakthrough approach. The basic series progresses through six books, usefully identified by their colours – red, green, blue, yellow, violet and orange – and becoming progressively more suited to the more fluent young reader. At each level auxiliary readers give additional practice, and an increase in vocabulary. Supplementary readers, also colour-coded, give a further range of stories linked to the basic readers. There is thus 'horizontal spread' as well as vertical development in readability.

The story content is typically fanciful, and as such relates little to the real-life experience of the children. The initial sentence structures vary, some being rather 'forced' to suit criteria of simplicity and repetition. The stiltedness and triviality will be obvious from extracts quoted in later chapters. Whether they are more familiar in any sense to one kind of child rather than another seems a moot point. Whatever the adult reader may think of the texts, however, the children who began to use the scheme, in both the school being studied and in others observed for comparison purposes, seemed to enjoy it. They liked the illustrations, the colours and the stories, and some even enjoyed the repetition when reading aloud. The only complaints made were when children did not manage to move through a book quickly enough for their liking. This was typically found with the slower learners at times when the text was proving rather hard going.

In addition to the main approaches just outlined, the school also encouraged the children to look at books from a wide range in the classrooms and in the school library, making library sessions a regular activity. This whetted the appetite for some, and at the very least provided some insight into the variety of available children's literature – a very important matter if such insight was not being obtained elsewhere. Even the non-readers learned and gained pleasure from looking at the illustrations.

A further matter of policy was the use of the Gay Way work books and the Morris Language in Action materials with children who could read and write well enough to tackle the language 'puzzles' involved. These activities were enjoyed, and seemed to help those who were already beginning to read to think more about the structure of language. Whether this helped their reading is hard to say. The materials proved useful as diagnostic devices when exploring the children's various subskills in attempting to read.

Within this overall policy of provision of materials and approaches each teacher made a sustained effort to guide the whole class and to provide individual attention for each child. The difficulties and abilities of each child were carefully looked for, and help was given as it seemed needed – and needed it was, for most of the children were not quick learners and (in the case of reading) had little learning opportunity at home. Some aspects of their classroom experience of reading and writing during their first three years in school can now be described.

THE FIRST YEAR

During their first year in school the children were visited during the second and third terms when they were just 5 years old. In all there were twenty-three children in the class.

When observation was begun they had already been introduced to the *Breakthrough to Literacy* materials. The initial sample of words was displayed in a large wall-hung folder, and was used in short word learning and sentence building sessions conducted by the teacher. Various picture-books and the first Ladybird books were available on a stand for children to look at when directed to do so, or when they felt like looking at a book during free play activities.

The class sessions were conducted with the children seated in a group on a mat in front of the teacher, who had the Breakthrough sentence-stand beside her. This stand was slotted to take individual word cards which could stand alone or be arranged in a sentence. In a typical session, a week or two after the introduction, a child would volunteer to build a sentence from a small pool of words already used. As a word was placed on the stand some of the other children spontaneously recognised it, spoke it aloud and anticipated the next. It was difficult to know whether the child who was building the sentence was finally guided by his own initial intentions or by the other children's suggestions. When he had completed his building the teacher asked him what the sentence was, and, after checking it, asked other children to identify individual words. For the sentence *I see a television* she asked, for example, which was *see* and which was *I*. Another sentence built by a child was *I see my dad*. In each case, after the words *I* and *see* were identified several times by different children, the teacher asked the whole class to repeat the whole sentence in unison. Then individual children were asked to repeat it and their omissions and errors were corrected. Correct readings and suggestions were warmly approved and there were no overtones of criticism of children making mistakes.

On a later occasion, still in January, the sentence-frame *I play with* . . . was being used. When a child suggested a sentence for which words were not already available in the Breakthrough scheme the teacher wrote each required word on a new card and added it to the Breakthrough display. The children suggested *I play with my teddy-bear* and *I play with my doll's pram*. This latter provided an opportunity to use the individual letter *s* which is given as a separate item in the Breakthrough scheme to allow for plural number and possessive case building. It also invited the introduction of the idea of a *letter* with a corresponding *sound*. The children gave the impression at this point of responding very differently to the problem. Some seemed to be getting the idea, but instead of the unperturbed expressions characteristic of most of the children while the first sentence was being built, there appeared signs of uncertainty, unease and withdrawal. Presumably this was likely to happen at each point when a new idea was introduced, for expressions of ease were associated with familiar activities, whether or not their implications were grasped.

From early February other single letters were introduced in these class sessions, their forms were traced and their associated sounds were practised. On one occasion *m* and *c* were being learned. When sounding the letters the children were encouraged to frame their lips or mouths appropriately to maintain the sound rather than to produce a sharp, plosive version. This enabled the teacher to introduce the idea of words beginning with *m* and *c*, by setting the children to pronounce the sounds as though beginning a word. Some of them were then able to suggest appropriate words and to enjoy the game. A week later they were learning *h* and on this occasion one child suggested *hat*, but then, instead of offering examples beginning with *h* as the teacher seemed to intend, another child offered *cat*. The teacher then moved with this new direction and soon the children offered *mat*, *sat* and *rat*. The letters *c* and *m* had already been taught, but *s* and *r* were spontaneous suggestions, related perhaps to the earlier experience with a plural and to acquaintance with the word *rat* in other classroom reading materials (the Gay Way books). Obviously some children were responding to the analytic approach involved in combining both visual and phonic elements. Others were becoming aware of the idea of a letter while yet others were still grappling with the ideas of words and sentences. Sentence building with the Breakthrough materials was continued throughout this period of introduction to 'sounding' letters. Major advantages of the class sessions appeared to be the sense of unity and co-operation engendered, the ensuring that no child failed to be introduced to new aspects of reading skill, and the reminders of some of their basic work to those who were advancing in skill. There were obvious and compelling reasons, however, for intensive individual and small group work. This was based on each child's performance in various subskills. Pre-reading work included such activities as pattern tracing, pattern copying, labelling of pictures drawn by the children, looking at the pictures and lay-out of picture-books, and the recognition of names of objects and of the children's own names.

As some children began to recognise a few words and to copy reasonably well they were seated at a separate table apart from those who were still at the pre-reading stage. They were given personal Breakthrough folders in which they stored those words they used in sentence building in the group or individually with the teacher. Sometimes the teacher required them to build a particular sentence, and sometimes to suggest their own. For those who learned more rapidly she provided a personal sentence-book in which she wrote each sentence the child could build and might copy reasonably well by himself. By early March some of these children were judged to be ready to be introduced to the Gay Way reading scheme.

At this stage, therefore, the class was divided into three groups for reading activities. There were still the pre-readers whose word learning and copying skills were as yet very poor. There were the early readers who were working with different levels of success with the Breakthrough folders, some of whom might find word memory difficult but be fairly good at immediate visual and copying skill, some whose skills were in the reverse direction and yet others who were making little progress on either front. There was also the more advanced group who were ready to develop from their Breakthrough skills.

For this latter group the teacher prepared materials for introductory exercises for the Gay Way Red Book. She made small booklets containing illustrations cut from old copies and accompanied by carefully printed copies of phrases, which would prepare them for the sentences in the book proper. She also had illustrated cards which could be both read and copied. The first stage, however, was to introduce words like *hill*, *red* and *lorry* into Breakthrough folders which already contained words such as *the*, *went*, *little* and *up* which figured in the Gay Way text. Thus the children could move from their sentence building skills to cope with the new scheme. They seemed to find the illustrations, which were not a feature of Breakthrough, an added pleasure. By the end of March some of the children had their own copies of the Red Book and were able to read from them.

During the summer term the picture changed little except that some of the initial readers began to work with Gay Way materials while the more advanced readers moved from the Red Book series, to the Green and even to the Blue. This progress required more than word memory skills, especially at the Blue Book stage, and much of the individual work with better readers was directed towards checking their reading with understanding, improving their fluency and encouraging analytic skills (both visual and phonic) in attempting new words. A record of progress for each child was the book-marker carrying a list of pages read with the teacher. It was interesting to note the friendly spirit of co-operation and competition that developed among the more advanced readers. The way children took up reading activities, and developed them at such different rates, meant that at the end of the year an enormous gap had opened up between the better readers and those who had made virtually no start. While it was possible that the teacher's grouping practice had tended to confirm and enhance differences, it seemed to the observer that she had maintained sufficient contact with all the children to be flexible in her treatment of them and open to evidence of change in their interest and learning. Independent exploration of the skills of the ten selected children gave no grounds for thinking that, except for possible minor variations, her expectations and treatment were asking either more or less of any of the children than was based on a reasonable assessment of what they might be able to do. She was well aware, however, that all the children might have benefited from more time to look at books with her and to try to read to her.

In the light of the questions being asked in this study several points are worth noting. In so far as the act of writing might be understood, the children were given little to go on. Initially words were presented to be read, but the children had not seen them being written and could have no idea of a person behind them. When they did see words being written by the teacher the purpose of the act was not to communicate to anyone, but to add to the store of Breakthrough words. It may have simply looked like putting another decoration on the wall. Children's own manipulations of words on cards were more like a jigsaw puzzle activity than a communication task, and their own writing was developed in this context. In other words, the act of writing to have an effect on another person was never apparent.

As to the development of knowledge about the spelling system, two points can be made. The actions of naming letters (whether by phonic or other labelling techniques) drew attention to words as ordered strings of discrete letters. Unless the children gained experience of attending to a useful enough array to make comparisons, they had little opportunity to become acquainted with spelling patterns in the language.

THE SECOND YEAR

For their second year in school, during which they reached their sixth birthdays, the ten children were allocated to two classes. In both classrooms the Breakthrough wall folder, and illustrations of pictures and words from the Gay Way book were permanent features of wall-hung displays.

Early in the autumn term some of the children were observed looking at their Gay Way books and taking turns to read a little to the teacher. After a while she read a story to the whole class. One interesting observation was the way one of the children, who was not able to read at all and whose home experience lacked the handling of books, treated books like bricks, building a tower with them.

The two classes were again observed later in the term. In one there was first a session of class activity, working with the teacher on the phonic pattern -*ad*. Examples such as *bad*, *lad* and *dad* were used. The better readers found the work easy and were quite at home with it, others seemed to be attentive and following it, while others looked willing but rather lost. They were being shown an explicit analytic approach to pattern in written symbols. The experience itself was not as strange as it had been earlier. After this session the children sat at their tables for individual activities in their learning groups. These included sentence building and writing. Each child would supply a sentence which he tried to build from his Breakthrough sentence-maker, then, when it was complete (with teacher guidance where necessary), the teacher wrote it in the child's writing-book and the child then copied it. Exceptions were made for those children who could not yet build sentences, and for them the teacher wrote the sentence first. They then tried to copy it, and possibly to build it. One of the difficulties with which children helped each other was that of finding desired words in their sentence-makers. Small cards sometimes slipped behind others, or deep in the pockets, and could not easily be seen. One felt, when observing this activity, that all the children might benefit from individual uninterrupted help over a period of ten or twenty minutes, but this would require a totally different provision of teachers to pupils. The teacher's individual attention and attention to groups was obviously invaluable, but there was evidence of uncompleted activity and unsolved problems for most of the children. After this session the class again regrouped, as for a story, but this time they discussed a series of pictures with the teacher.

In the other class the children were at first engaged in individual and group play activities. One child was quite active and talkative with a group of girls playing a 'guess the word' game with Breakthrough cards. She had no idea of the words, and neither had the others to any great extent, but the self-appointed leader seemed to know enough to keep the party going. The game, rather than the words, seemed to be the thing! For the final part of the morning the class was engaged as a group in discussion with the teacher. Some were attentive and involved (in a quiet way) for most of the time. Others were quite chatty, making spontaneous comments, but one or two looked very tired and their attention wandered before long. At one point one girl reached out to touch the teacher as though expressing some need to convey contact and warmth. Another sat quietly and tried to fit in with the activity, but her attention seemed to wane. When the teacher asked a question and said, 'Put your hands up', this child raised hers as if she were simply obeying an instruction. It is doubtful whether she knew the answer, or even that a question had been asked.

After the Christmas holidays the classes were again visited before individual children were interviewed. In one most children were working in their number-books from work cards. These latter had pictures of simple objects like trees and cherries and printed words such as *draw 6 cherries*. The children had to copy the writing and draw freehand the appropriate number of items. Other cards had an array of pictures of different items and the words *How many?*. Here the task was to copy the words, supply the number and draw copies of the pictured items by drawing round appropriate plastic shapes which were provided. Children unable to do this were given tasks with peg boards and counters. After about twenty minutes the teacher changed the activities. Some children played with jigsaws and plasticine, while others worked with their sentence-makers and writing-books. The teacher concentrated on listening to individual children reading from their Gay Way books, and later the whole class listened to a story. In the other class the children were given various activities to carry out by themselves while the teacher devoted her time to listening to individual children reading. Some of the girls played their flash card game. Some made wild guesses at the words and were less successful than the others, and one at least thought that any word would do! This class, too, had a story to finish the morning.

Intermittent observations of classroom activity during the rest of the year suggested that both classes were settled into their own characteristic activities and atmosphere, with a sense of stability about the daily rhythm of school life. The feeling that new activities could be expected was set in an air of familiarity with the classroom, the teacher, each other and many of the materials which provided the backbone of reading and number work schemes. The classrooms had, by the third term, the richly decorated look of displays of children's work and of items of interest on 'nature tables', as well as the book displays in 'library' corners, the storage shelves of paints and brightly coloured materials, and the fuller array of Breakthrough words in the wall folders. The teachers fostered much individual and group work, but also drew the classes together for general administrative reasons, for television viewing, physical activities, story-telling, singing and for short instruction sessions using demonstration and question-and-answer techniques.

A final session was spent in one class when the children were seated at their tables engaged in writing activities. No longer were the less able writers copying patterns; all were attempting words, phrases, or more complex productions. Some children were not very successful in their attempts to copy words and to illustrate them, although they seemed to enjoy using paper, pencils and crayons, and showed their work to seek approval and help. One task was to copy Gay Way sentences from printed cardboard strips and to illustrate them. One child wrote *I am the fat pig* correctly enough but without spacing the words and with a very shaky hand. Another copied *It is a red lorry* in a small, wobbly hand and with a reversed *a*, but it was readable and showed some word spacing. Both tended to read what they had written in terms only of the final noun phrases *fat pig* and *a red lorry*, suggesting that they remembered what the sentences were about rather than actually reading them. Illustration would, of course, increase this tendency. Both children took a long time to copy, but did persist with the task.

Another group were copying individual words from separate cards with appropriate illustrations. This was likely to help the children to learn new words, but it was clear that they could often not read all their own words back – and this was not because the writing was too poor, for it was in fact quite readable. One child had listed *box*, *top*, *wig*, *fish*, *web*, *hand*, *sun* and *lid,* without spacing them but with no errors. He had trouble reading them back, however, for he could not match all of them with his own drawings. Another had a similar list written in quite a clear well-formed hand, but again without confidence in knowing what she had written. It was clear that further practice was needed to consolidate the learning.

The better readers were using their Breakthrough folders, now well stocked with words, to build their own sentences before writing them. One was working on *My mum and me went to the hospital last night,* and she wrote this in a firm, neat hand with good spacing. Previous sentences in her writing book included *In my house I have got a dog*: *We have had some rock which Erica bought for us*; and *I am a girl and I am six.* She obviously commanded a variety of sentence structures in her speech. A boy was working on *It is my brother's birthday*, and he wrote it with quite fair spacing but a very uneven hand. He made no errors. Previous sentences included *I am going to get some new pumps tomorrow*, but on the whole their structure was very limited. This boy's writing was more restricted than either his speech or his reading, possibly because he knew his untidy effort was not his best work. He might have benefited from some careful checking of the precise way he formed his letters. Another girl had been writing sentences like *It is sunny and hot again today* in a neat hand and with adequate spacing.

Only two children were much more advanced. They were writing paragraphs freely. One wrote: *Tomorrow I am going to Town and I am getting some new shoes And a Ginger Bread Man and a Bag of Sweets And some Dinner And food. And then we went home.* In spite of the punctuation problems there were no spelling errors. The other child wrote an even longer piece about a visit to her grandmother. She had few punctuation problems and kept to the past tense presentation, but had spelling errors such as *Grammars* for *Grandma's*, *ther* for *there*, *wen* for *when*, *super* for *supper*. Her sentence construction included *when* clauses and embedded conjunction with *and*, as in *I went home and had my tea* . . ..

Meanwhile in the other class the children were observed doing number work at their tables. Some were writing and completing short sums as set out on the blackboard, for example $5 + 4 = $. The children doing this kind of work at this table were calculating by using small plastic unit bricks which slotted together into a row. For the given example the idea was to slot a set of five together, then a set of four and then to combine them and count the total. This was not always done, however, the additional sum being slotted one at a time on to the original with all the consequent errors of forgetting how many! But the children seemed to be grasping the general idea and to be enjoying their task. Children in the more advanced group had completed this number task and were working on Gay Way work books – sets of word recognition and analysis problems related to the Gay Way scheme. A few children were threading beads and copying items like *Draw 2 shells* and drawing the appropriate number of objects.

After their number work the children listened to a story, and the opportunity was taken of looking at some of their recent writing. One child had been copying phrases, but her writing was not always recognisable and was always very wobbly. She had written *pot house*, for example, with two *t*s to *pot*, a reversed *u* in *house* and a final *e* wrapped obscurely around the *s*. (She was not yet able to recognise and read any of the words she could copy.) Another, however, wrote clearly and with well-spaced words. His writing was characterised by an odd raising of the letter *g* so that the tail rested on a level with the lower parts of letters like *o*, *i*, and so on, and with the enclosed upper portion level with the tops of letters like *h* and *l*. He was able to write his own freely produced sentences and a recent paragraph was: *One day a little girl went for a walk and found a little dog wot cut his poor. She tuk the dog home and began to cut the bandage and she cut a finger and they lived HAPPY agen.* This showed a curious mixture of accurate spelling of words for which he had a model, and of his own 'phonetic' versions of those which he had to invent. Given his slow reading relative to that of others his writing was perhaps surprisingly advanced.

It was noted during the first year that little was done to help the children understand the communicative function of writing. This also seemed true of the second year. (Evidence that at least one child had no notion was her view that the appropriate response to a written word was to say any word that came into her head!) Classroom tasks presented writing as reporting or copying rather than a primary act of expression. Copying words and sentences served the useful purpose of developing handwriting and increasing exposure to words to be learned, but any 'message' was largely irrelevant. This impression must have been intensified by its being set in the larger framework of copying patterns and drawing pictures. The experience of authorship was mediated from spoken sentences through sentence building with ready-made words, the actual act of writing being a report or recording of what had been said. This feeling that writing was a representation of a message already conveyed was intensified by the way it was used to record number work and other classroom activity. If any child had asked why the teacher or the children were writing things everybody knew about, his question would have been justified.

Nevertheless, some children had gained insight, and some of their writing seemed to be enlivened by a genuine communicative intent. Perhaps they also sensed an author behind the stories they read in their books, but that any of them should ever think that someone really wanted to tell them that the little red lorry went up the hill stretches belief.

As in the first year, little in the teaching drew attention to English spelling as a system, though the move into phonic blending to treat digraphs as units might have helped. Here, however, it should not be forgotten that in the previous year children's responses to some of the invitations to suggest similar words to one on the board had not followed the teacher's intention of tracing simple letter similarity, but had suggested awareness of digraph pattern.

THE THIRD YEAR

In their third year of schooling the eight children who remained of the original ten were brought together into one class. They had a male teacher for the first time in their school lives, and, though not for this reason, a slightly more formal organisation of their activities. Yet the classroom atmosphere was one of a warm and friendly discipline. Whenever the class was observed the children were either working at various tasks seated in groups round their tables, or were involved as a whole class in teacher-directed activities, including listening to stories, talking about various topics with blackboard or other illustration or models, and engaging in question-and-answer exchanges about specific teaching points in the areas of numeracy and literacy. Less formal activity took place at

other times of day, while for music, dancing, PE, watching television and library reading the children went to other rooms.

The teacher grouped the children at five tables according to their
reading and number abilities. When first observed both the first and
second groups were practising writing by copying from books, and
were attempting comprehension exercises from a work-book. The
children were able to work alone, but they also exchanged questions, advice and comments about each other's work and behaviour.
At the third and fourth tables, children were building sentences in
the Breakthrough folders under the teacher's supervision, and copying them into their exercise-books. At the fifth table they were occupied with simple number work materials, jigsaws and introductory
Gay Way picture cards.

A second observation session after half-term showed some
change in the classroom arrangement. By now evidence of completed classwork was displayed around the room and on the walls.
Vivid pictures of bonfire night were interspersed with specimens of
successful writing, while interesting models were arranged on tables
by the walls. Most, if not all, children had some item on show, or
had shared in a production. The children were now seated at pairs of
tables at three ability levels. When observed they were working
from the Sound Sense series of books by A. E. Tansley and
published by E. J. Arnold. When they had finished the exercises set
for them they handed in their books and went on to drawing, tracing
and reading with the Language in Action resource books developed
by Joyce Morris and published by Macmillan. There was a pleasant,
well-controlled atmosphere with touches of humour from the
teacher that were appreciated by the children. Children working
from Book Four of the Sound Sense series were tackling exercises
such as copying sentences and then underlining *ar* in words like
farmer, park, dark, and choosing the right word in multiple choice
tasks such as *She had a basket on her (arm, leg, home)* and *Here (is,
are, arm) the cakes for the (start, party, garden)*. They understood
the nature of the tasks, but tackled them rather differently. One
made a sensible choice of words where required, and underlined
appropriately. Her writing was a comfortable size, but was erratic in
line and in the formation of letters. Nevertheless, words were well
spaced, capitals were used correctly and the work was error-free.
Another was equally able, but was careless with his copying. He
substituted words in sentences as though he were not directly
copying but reproducing a reading as, for example, in *The farmer
feeds the sheep* for *The farmer feeds his sheep*. His actual writing was
very erratic and very tiny, but he did not mis-spell. Yet another
found the task more difficult because he did not successfully read all

the sentences. Both his choice of suitable words and his copying showed error. In one case, *It was late and we were (are, car, far) from home,* he copied correctly but chose *car,* while for *She had a basket on her (arm, leg, home)* he wrote *She add a bask in a ham.* His writing was neat and well formed, so it seemed his difficulty in not getting the gist of some of the sentences affected his attention in the copying.

A child who was working from Book Two of the Sound Sense series was finding words with *oo* in a set of sentences and writing them in her book, and then copying sentences like *The m – – n was in the sky,* inserting the missing letters. She produced well-copied sentences in clear, firm writing of a good size, and completed the tasks successfully. She might well have been more successful than the third child mentioned above if she had tried his tasks, but his inclusion in the upper ability group was based on more than his reading. At another table children were using Book One and were identifying items in a picture represented by words with an *i.* Suitable words were already in print in the book, and selection was not difficult. Nevertheless, the task of writing the chosen words required identification and copying. One child managed to find eight words, and copied them correctly, but his writing was over-large and erratic, especially in alignment. Another copied seven suitable words, six correctly, but with reversals of both letters *s* in *sails.* His writing was a good size, the word spacing was good, and the words sat reasonably well on the line of the exercise-book. Yet another, at the same table, was not asked to work from a Sound Sense book, but was copying a story from one of the Language in Action books. The heading was copied rather erratically, and the first line reasonably well, in writing of a good size, but subsequent lines were overwritten and unreadable. Inspection of his book showed other instances of work beginning clearly but soon degenerating into spidery, erratic, and unreadable writing. At this stage he was experiencing some difficulty with his vision.

One problem facing the teacher throughout the year was the slow progress made in basic skills. Although the two more able groups were developing reasonably well, two-thirds of the class were not, and one-third seemed to make scarcely any headway. Any progress in most of the children required considerable consolidation. It was scarcely surprising, then, that the Breakthrough approach was still much in evidence in the classroom, even in this third year. By January, and through the second term, an array of envelopes containing cardboard strips with the basic Breakthrough vocabulary extended along the lower half of one wall. Regular sentence building was a feature of classroom work, the children in the slow learning groups being expected to learn to identify the word printed on an envelope and to extract a strip to help construct a suggested sentence. Yet those who were better readers also had evidence of their ability hanging on the wall, for now some of the pictures were accompanied by written commentary. One had three quite full sentences; others showed more complex construction than had previously been used; and more advanced vocabulary (for example, *machinery*) was appearing. The range of ability, combined with the heavy weighting towards slow learners, presented problems which could only be met by skilful teaching in conditions which allowed the teacher to attend to individuals or groups as necessary.

Observing the children in the classroom from time to time during the three years was invaluable for this study. It gave the children a sense of sharing school experience with the observer, and the latter a basis for understanding the children's comments and behaviours in tests and interviews. It also provided the possibility of answering some questions relating to their learning.

First, how far did the teachers' expectations influence their treatment of the pupils? One thing was clear. Any prior expectations could not be applied at first to individual children. In general the teachers expected, from past experience, that learning might be a slow business for a number of the children, and that some would learn rather well in spite of unpromising home conditions; but they could only find out about particular children as time passed. Early assessments, moreover, could be modified, especially since the timing of making some step in learning might not be related to the rate of further progress. Thus children did not hold constant rankings relative to each other, and various strengths and weaknesses yielded individual profiles rather than overall estimates of ability for each child. The reason why the sample children retained a fairly constant relative ordering with regard to reading was that they spanned the total range and emerging differences were quite substantial.

Secondly, some idea could be gained from classroom observation as to how representative the sample children were of the total intake with respect to activities and abilities not assessed by means of tests. It was useful to know, for instance, that more children at 7 could read 'outside the reading scheme' than might have been estimated from the single instance in the sample of ten. Similarly some of the children could write, and write short 'stories', better than any of the sample children.

Thirdly, observation was useful in checking the ways reading was approached. There is often a difference between the methods advocated by authors of reading schemes and those actually used by teachers. The most informative report of the background to children's learning combines description of scheme materials with an account of how they are used. In this case, teachers' reports of what was happening were usefully checked by seeing how they went about their task and how the children actually behaved in response to their efforts. It was also useful to try to check whether the teachers' methods were more supportive of some children than others. What could be concluded was that no sample child suffered from a relative lack of attention to himself or to his learning, though whether any child might have done better with different guidance could not be ascertained. The teachers were well aware of this question and welcomed discussion of their task.

Further interpretation of the children's behaviour in various tasks with the observer outside the classroom could be better evaluated in the light of their classroom activity, particularly when questions of shyness, lack of response and unfamiliarity with tasks were involved. For example, the quality of certain children's relative lack of verbal response was better judged when their individual behaviours with the teacher and other children were also seen.

Finally it was possible to gain a general impression of the children's understanding of the nature of reading and writing and of their learning about English spelling in the context of the ways they were taught. The comments made after the report of the first and second years' observations were not modified in the light of the third. Reading and writing had by then become necessary skills across the curriculum, number work in particular being embedded in literacy, but the importance of writing as an art of communication was something many of the children were slowly discovering by themselves. Similarly, awareness of English orthography was more evident, but again was an emergent knowledge. Would suitably guided discovery have helped some of the children to learn with less difficulty? Detailed analysis of the performance of the sample children was expected to throw light on the complexities of learning.

Note: On the following pages certain conventions are adopted in transcripts of children's reading, i.e.:

*   Help provided by adult, usually whole word.

( )   Misreadings and attempts to correct them.

− − −   Separate soundings of letters to attempt a reading.

Chapter 4

The Successful Readers

Of the children selected for detailed study only John and Wilma were reading at or beyond the norm by the time they were 7. In the following accounts the children are first introduced and then their understanding of reading and writing is explored. This is inferred from conversations with the children, an interview with their mothers, and from observations of relevant behaviours. The structured interviews outlined in Tests A4 and B7 (Appendix A and Appendix B) yielded useful data. The second part of each account is a discussion of their knowledge of English spelling, set in the context of the general development of their reading skills.

JOHN

John's mother was interviewed towards the end of his second year in school and it might first be helpful to draw on her account together with information given by the school. The child entered school as a sturdy, healthy, energetic 5-year-old. He attended school regularly, and appeared to have no vision or hearing problems. He was the first of two children of a father who worked for a painting and decorating firm and a mother who worked as a tailoress. His maternal grandmother lived with the family. John received a great deal of care and attention from his family, being regarded by them as a bright child, and he had developed a confident and rather self-assertive manner. In any confrontation with another child he was not at a loss for either physical or verbal means of defending himself, and, in general he was inclined to adopt a dominant role. At first he was very responsive and co-operative, but as he found his feet in school he began to be a nuisance and to need some firm control. His attitude began to suggest that he did not think school activities worth pursuing; but he did in fact make good progress with his reading and managed to learn effectively in spite of his 'front'. Whether the arrival of a younger brother during John's first year at school was one of the factors behind his restless behaviour could not really be determined, but it seemed likely that he had some considerable adjustment to make.

His mother said that he had always appeared to be bright and 'pressing to know' even as a toddler. He had pressed for help with reading but done much of the work himself. He used to read shop signs before he went to school and asked for help with them. He had not asked much, however, for anyone to read to him. Nevertheless, his mother had read him stories, especially when he was about 5; so had his father and grandmother. She judged that at 7 this was no longer appropriate. During his school years he had read aloud to her and to others, but at 7 he read by himself. A typical home reading activity referred to by his mother was reading the *TV Times* in order to plan his viewing. The overall picture given by both John and his mother was not of a child who liked to sit down and read story-books to any great extent, but rather of one who read avidly whatever was important to him at the time. This might on occasion be a story-book, such as the *Monsters and Ghosts* book he was currently enjoying. But it could equally well be any information displayed in the environment, his current comic, or adult literature which caught his attention. An important feature was that he read not only for pleasure but also for information.

When interviewed about reading after he had just reached 5, John said that he could not yet read, and that he was learning in order to read the Red Book. He could describe some of its contents and he spoke of having a TV comic at home. He anticipated reading like his grandmother when he was bigger, saying that she read a lot of books. His father read the newspapers and his mother read library books, though John spoke rather disparagingly of the latter. He reported that both parents read to him at home, as did his grandmother who read to him nearly every night. He himself tried to read aloud to them, especially to his mother. He claimed that he was finding the Red Book easy and could not identify anything hard about it. He read the first sentence easily, but stalled fractionally over the second before suddenly recalling all of it. He said he knew what it said because he 'thought in his head'. He found pictures helpful, and if he encountered a word he did not know he would try to remember or ask the teacher. These observations suggested that John's strategies were to seek sense rather than graphic accuracy, and to depend on recall rather than new analysis. He sensed that it was up to the reader to make something of written material, and was familiar with written signs and messages of various kinds in the environment at home, in school and in his urban world. But at this stage the act of reading was simply one of remembering what had previously been learned. His view of writing was dominated by the experience in school of copying sentences constructed by himself or the teacher with Breakthrough materials. Writing followed sentence construction through manipulation of cards – it was not a primary experience. The nearest John came to indicating awareness of the direct communicative significance of writing and reading was mention of shopping lists.

From this point on John's reading developed well, but his writing did not. In spite of initially good performance on copying tasks, his later work was untidy and poorly formed. The suspicion that this was possibly not a problem of poor motor control, but a declaration of impatience, was intensified early in his second year. His classwork at this stage indicated a strong interest in number work. His efforts to draw and label geometric shapes, and to write instructions like *Draw 3 cherries*, were tidier and more legible than expected when his number work-book was compared with his writing-book. Perhaps John responded better if he felt he was writing to some purpose, and simply copying Breakthrough materials had not seemed sensible to him.

It was most interesting to find that at the end of his third year he responded to the efforts of a teacher who conveyed better than the others that she was really interested in what he personally could write. The result was spontaneous writing much more in keeping with his reading ability. By this time, when interviewed, he conveyed enjoyment of reading both at home and at school, he was well able to explore the wide choice of books available in school, and he was aware of library provision in the neighbourhood.

With a growing understanding of the nature of the art of reading when he entered school, John was set fair to learn to read. No language problem seemed likely to inhibit him since he was able to communicate well over tasks in the classroom, he could tell a simple coherent story, he could explain and consider possible as well as actual states of affairs, and he scored well on the picture vocabulary test. Dialect, which some might have considered to be a handicap, did not appear to present any difficulty. Indeed, if anything, reading seemed to modify his speech when telling a story. The following example of a story task – not his best narrative since he had listened restlessly – shows how dialect met standard English in a particular manner of speaking. It should be compared with the model in Test B4 (Appendix B), where the story is seen not to begin with 'Once upon a time'.

Once upon a time there was an elephant called Jumbo and a kangaroo. The kangaroo said 'I've got to have a tooth out. My friend had some magic teeth. And when he had it out he just put it straight under his pillow. And in the morning he found a silver fivepence under his pillow'. And then the kangaroo had to go for one. And then he put one under his pillow. And then he found a fivepence under his pillow the next morning. Jumbo weren't a kangaroo! And then he run downstairs and creeped out like a mouse. And then he shown the kangaroo the tooth he got. The thing he got were the fivepence.

To trace John's developing knowledge of English spelling a chronological account of his performance in various tasks and in reading aloud will be used. The first relevant information came from Tests A2 and A3 (Appendix A) in his second term in school, when he was just 5. He could distinguish letters from numbers and could name some of both. The letters were those he had been taught to name 'phonically' in school. He seemed to understand the terms *letter* and *sentence* fairly well, but to be less sure about *word*. In class he knew seven of the Breakthrough words and also knew of *house* and *home,* but confused them. By the end of that term, in March, he could write a reasonable version of *I am a boy*, knowing what it meant and what each word 'said', from memory. He also suggested, and successfully wrote, one or two other short sentences he had come across in his classwork.

Test A4 (Appendix A) revealed that he had formed some idea of what did not constitute a sentence in English, but his ideas were clearly based on a limited experience of *written* forms. He judged *Ben is a dog* and *I am a boy* to be sentences, but rejected *is Ben a dog* and *Ben dog a is* on the grounds that they did not start with *The*, and *am I a boy* and *boy am a I* because they did not start with *I*. This was in spite of a correct oral reading of all of them. His rules for sentences were not based on spoken English but were that they had to begin with certain words. Inspection of his classwork showed that he was using twenty-eight Breakthrough words in his sentence-maker, and had written thirteen different sentences in his writing-book, but all began with *I*.

This 'pattern perception' approach to sentences was also reflected in his reading of words, where similar letter patterns led to confusion. Although he could not read the words he judged *down* and *have* to be dissimilar, but *house* and *home* to be alike. When asked, he pointed to *h*, *o* and *e* as what was the same about them. In class and in Test A5 (Appendix A) he also confused *boy* with *baby*, *dog* with *big* and *in* with *tin*. Altogether these misreadings, or miscues as they are sometimes called, suggested some implicit recognition of aspects of letter patterning in words.

Test A5 was attempted two months later, in the third term, when

John read all the sentences correctly and all the words except *baby*. When asked to do the further task of finding words hidden in others he noticed *dog* in *dogs*, *cat* in *cats*, *pin* in *pink*, *red* in *tired* and *red* and *is* in *redistribute*. This suggested considerable progress with orthographic knowledge, and achievement at a level that, from Soderbergh's study, would lead one to predict attempts at new words. But in spite of his success with this task, John was relatively less successful when reading from the Gay Way material. He made more errors than Wilma, for example, in sentences that were familiar to him from the Red Book, most of these being in the earlier rather than the later examples. It seemed possible that his visual memory was not always tapped as well as it might have been and that when learning to read new material he did not attend carefully enough to store it firmly in memory, and therefore found recent recall easier than more distant. His better grasp of the Breakthrough words was possibly due to the longer time spent with them, at a stage when attending to individual words was more a part of his experience than was moving through a reading book. With a reading book John seemed to read primarily for meaning, using only some of the visual cues, a strategy which may have limited his attention to the graphic patterns. His reading of Gay Way word lists was clearly less good than that of the familiar sentences, and very comparable with his reading of reordered but meaningful sentences. Thus without the familiar context his word recognition was not so good. It was even weaker with mixed sentences where meanings derived from different familiar sentences were combined into a new 'idea'. John's actual misreadings included graphic confusions between *pots* and *pans*, *on* and *no*, and *down* and *went*, but his chief source of error was failure to attempt in different contexts words that he read correctly in the familiar sentences. But every correct reading strengthened his appreciation of spelling pattern, and in the classroom, as distinct from test situations, he was steadily increasing his range of familiar words in familiar contexts.

At about this time he began to try sounding the first letter of words he could not recall or had not met. This was a response to classroom teaching of naming letters phonically, and to trying to encourage children to mouth initial letters according to their phonic names and to attempt to blend them and continue the mouthing into the complete saying of the word. Although John grasped this quickly, he only found it useful when he attempted it with some of the words he had met before, and with new words when their remainder was visually very similar to, or identical with, a word he already knew. In other words, elementary phonics were only useful to him in the context of visual pattern recognition.

Later in the third term of his first year John's reading aloud from his 'reader' (now the Green Book) was recorded. He read restlessly as though he thought it a bit of a nuisance. The transcript follows, with phonic attempts hyphenated, help asterisked, and corrections and comments bracketed.

Jo ran back to the street. His little f-e-e-t, f-ee-t, feet went p-a-d, pad, pad, pad, pad, pad. Bang went the door. It shut on the old street-cat. Meow, meow, meow, meow, meow*. (one too many) I am shut out* of the house. Meow, meow, meow. I have no house to live in. I have no rug to sit on, and I have no garden. (Age 5 years 2 months)

It was obvious that John had little trouble with this reading, and was rather impatient with it. His comprehension was good in that he answered questions correctly without the book, although his initial reaction was to want to look at the book. He seemed surprised to be asked, and possibly more interested than at any other time in the interview. In spite of the relatively easy nature of the material for him at that stage (he was soon to be reading the Blue Book) there was evidence, when he was unsure, both of phonic attack and of graphic comparison. The new word *pad* was sounded successfully, and *feet* was attempted with two separate open *e*s. When asked, however, what happens when two *e*s come together he immediately said *ee like street-cat* and sounded *f-ee-t*, *feet* correctly. The extra *meow* and the help with *out*, which amounted to showing him he had missed it, were probably symptomatic of his tendency to dash through the reading. In a later joint interview with Wilma with the Second Blue Book it was noticed that he was quick to guess a new word by sentence context if sounding did not yield the answer, managing both *shoe* and *inside* in this way.

By the end of his first year in school John was working quite successfully through the Gay Way reading scheme. He tended to guess new words from the meaning of what he had already read, but sometimes his phonic naming of initial letters helped him in this, as did recognition of letter patterns which reminded him of similar words and thus of part of the visual and sound structure. Phonic naming of letters and recognition of patterns were still more useful, however, in reminding him of words he had come across before.

This interpretation of his reading skills was strengthened by his performance in Test B2 (Appendix B) early in his second year. The first tasks in the test seemed to John to be too easy to deserve concentration. He completed them adequately, but with a clear air of impatience, except when he created interest by counting letters to justify his choice of big and little words. The letter pattern recognition and matching challenged him, however, and while he found initial patterns and the central double-vowel pattern confidently enough, he had to work to find the final-letter pattern matches especially if a three-letter pattern was involved. He completed the oral sentences easily and interestingly. Overall, he seemed to have a good grasp of the word/letter distinction, and of graphic pattern recognition. He was well able to anticipate meaning and this seemed likely to be a strong point in his reading. At this stage he wrote very little spontaneously in class, but what he did write was spelled with very little error. His store of words for sentence construction in his Breakthrough folder was about a hundred, and he was able to read all thirty words in the Breakthrough Test A5 (Appendix A) easily and correctly.

A sample of John's reading in November from the Third Blue Book is given below. It can be compared with Wilma's since both children presented the same page to be read. Like Wilma, John was also required by the teacher to read easier texts for fluency, but he was rather nearer a fluent performance on this more difficult text than she was.

Extract from the Third Blue Book (Gay Way)
He sleeps and eats and sleeps and eats all day long.
What do you think he likes to eat?
He likes to eat the things that are four years old.

John's reading to observer (Age 5 years 7 months)
J: He sleeps and eats and sleeps and eats (a long day) all day long.
    What do you think he thinks* to eat?
O: Do you think that was right?
J: Yes . . . ate.
O: No. Try it again.
J: What do you think he thinks* to eat?
O: Do you think that's 'thinks'? (pointing to the word) Try to sound it.
J: l-i-k-s- . . . licks . . . leks . . . legs . . . I don't know that word.
O: Try 'i' (long) instead of 'i' (short), and make it sensible.
J: (likes) likes to eat.
    He likes to eat the . . . I don't know.
O: Try it.
J: I don't know it. (sound exasperated)

O: It starts with . . .?
J: (th . . ., thinks . . .) things that are four yes old.
O: Say that last bit again.
J: four years old.

When John hit a problem he was willing to try a phonic approach, but he was basically looking for sense, and disliked having to stop in the middle of a reading. When he tried a phonic breakdown he ranged over similar sounding words seeking one that fitted. This was particularly interesting; phonic sounding opened up a restricted set of possibilities rather than a single solution. There was little sign of graphic misreading, and it seemed that his reading had developed along the lines of complete word recognition, or recognition facilitated by phonic clues from recognised individual letters and from the gist of the content. Where necessary he could make a complete simple phonic synthesis quite quickly, and could even enjoy doing so as a problem task, whilst at the same time being impatient with the request to stop to do it while reading. He gave a distinct impression that his use of 'sounding' in reading was not a response to phonics instruction but a skill which was emergent from his abilities to name letters, to see letter patterns and to recognise a moderate range of words.

By December his reading had taken him a little further in the Third Blue Book. He read willingly, and his obvious competence led to a short sampling.

Extract from the Third Blue Book (Gay Way)
Next day he woke up and said, I am a very hungry crocodile. I am getting so thin. I must get my dinner, my four-year-old dinner. So he came out of the mud to look for his dinner. Jip the cat sat under a tree.

John's reading (Age 5 years 8 months)
Next day (the) he (walk) woke up and said, I am a very hungry crocodile. I am getting s . . . so thin. I must (go) get my dinner, my four-years-old dinner. So he came out of the mud to look for his dinner.
Jip the cat sat under (the) a tree.

Again he read quite fluently but not too carefully, though all his corrections were noticed and carried through without help, this time without any evidence of 'sounding'. He did not notice the use of *years* instead of *year*, and it was quite possible that he was using an expression familiar to him in everyday conversation. The errors seemed to be due to a rather slap-dash approach rather than any difficulty, but they did show graphic similarity to the correct words and semantic appropriacy in relation to the prior context. In the light of the earlier observation that his sounding sometimes led to a small range of possible words from which he found one that fitted the orthography and the sense, the errors he made here might well have been the result of a smoother, faster performance of that kind. In February a further reading was recorded as shown below:

Extract from the Third Blue Book (Gay Way) (Age 5 years 10 months)
You are getting so small, said Pat. You are so wet, said Pipkin. Drip, drip, drip, drip. Splash, splash, splash, splash. All day long the sun shone on Mr Snowman. All day long his snowball head got smaller and smaller. All day long his snowball body got smaller and smaller. All day long his snowball legs got smaller and smaller. Oh, Mr Snowman, you look very sad, said Pat.

A transcript seems unnecessary, for this was very smooth, with good intonation. John found the passage easy, especially with the repetition involved, and made no errors except for a reading of *are* for *look* in the last sentence. He corrected it immediately, obviously from the appearance of the word because the sense of either would stand. It was an example of an error of anticipation based on syntax and sense. Since the reading was so easy it was possible that John was not attending sufficiently to grasp the meaning, but when he was asked what was happening to the snowman he said it was melting. He was quite sure the word *melt* was in the text, and was most surprised when he tried to find it. He persisted in a word-by-word check because he was taken up with the question. Obviously he had read with understanding!

John's handwriting had consistently been untidy, and the sampling in the third term proved no exception. He wrote firmly and maintained a reasonably good line across the page; he spaced his words reasonably; he produced no reversals; but his letters were not regular or well formed. His spelling of his first name was correct, as was that of the sentences he copied. Unlike the other children he also produced a complete and correctly spelled version of the dictated sentence, and wrote two sentences of his own with scarcely any error. *I like my frend* (friend) and *My mum is kind* were, however, examples he had met previously in class.

Another smooth reading was sampled in June, this time from a school library book.

Extract from Monsters and Ghosts – *a book of stories* (Age 6 years 2 months)

Lots of the children said they had seen a large white something in the Junior School. They said it moved and was rather scaring. 'I think some of you who are big and brave should go together and find out about the ghost,' said Miss Grant.

Six boys went off together, but they were not away long. When they came back they laughed and laughed.

This was fluent and free from error. Because John was enjoying the reading he went on for several pages before he was stopped, falling foul of only one word – *mysterious*. This he read as *my stories,* but knew it did not fit the sense. Nor did his next attempt of *my sisters.* When the word *mystery* was written for him he read it correctly and then suggested *mysteries* for *mysterious.* He was helped with the ending, but did not know the word; yet he guessed it was like *exciting.* This suggested a good grasp of the syntax and sense of the sentence containing the word.

For most of his second year he had read without 'sounding', and in his third developed the art of silent reading. His reading aloud in November (this time from the Yellow Book in the Gay Way series) was smooth and error-free, and he comprehended the text well and said he liked the stories. He was also observed reading silently, and there was no sign of lip movement; but after this reading his comprehension seemed less sure, though a repetition of silent reading yielded better understanding. As a point of interest he also read aloud the blurb on the inside cover of the book, but while he read it successfully the meaning was not clear to him, and he was not keen to repeat the experience.

He did enjoy the 'foreign word' and *e*-cancelling tasks (C1, C2, Appendix C), however, and understood them and tackled them quickly. Although he did not sound any of the words in the judgement tasks, it should be remembered that his reading seemed to have taken him beyond that stage. He clearly recognised non-English letter patterns, saying that *dl*, *vl*, *hs*, and *gn* could not come together, but he was not sure whether to treat nonsense syllables as new English words or as foreign. In one task he treated them as 'made-up' English words, in another as non-English. This may well have been a conceptual problem rather than one of orthographic knowledge.

In the *e*-cancelling task (C3, Appendix C) his approach was rather cavalier (he cancelled only 39 per cent of the instances) but not random. The research literature suggests that some kind of phonic processing during silent reading might lead to 'silent *es*' being missed. John, however, omitted to cancel in all instances of *the* and in most final position *es*, including the 'silent' ones. This suggested a visual, rather than a phonic, processing.

Two further examples of his reading, both without error, fluent, and with good intonation and comprehension, are given below. The first was from a story-book read in February and the second from a newspaper reading in June. This latter was chosen because John could not decide what to read, and the observer had the daily paper to hand.

'Alas! That I have such a stupid woman for a wife!' grumbled the old man. 'Why should I live in this poor house, when I could be rich?'

The old woman stopped stirring the rice, and stared at her husband.

'How could you become rich?' she asked.

'When the rice rolls into the village, one grain rolls into each hut', said her husband.

'That is so,' agreed the woman.

'We have one hut,' said her husband 'therefore we have one grain of rice. If we had two huts, we should have two grains of rice. I shall build another hut, and sell the extra grain of rice in another village where it does not roll.' (Age 6 years 10 months)

Panda crashes
A police car carrying a badly wounded officer from the scene of a terrorist ambush crashed yesterday with a lorry on a lonely road in County Fermanagh.

The car was ambushed two miles from Rosslea on the road to Five Mile Town, near the Irish border. Three police officers in plain clothes were travelling in the vehicle, which was fired on and the driver hit in the right leg.

He managed to keep control of the car for about half a mile then stopped to let another officer take the wheel. Two miles further on, as the car rounded a double bend, it collided with the lorry.

The two officers not hurt in the ambush were both cut and bruised but were not kept in hospital. Their wounded colleague was being detained last night. (Age 7 years 2 months)

It was no wonder that the Daniels and Diack test proved easy for him, and that he also had no difficulty with its diagnostic subtests.

It was clear that John resembled Clark's young fluent readers in his active approach to reading, but he was not fluent before starting school, and he learned much during his first two years there. It was also clear that before he attended school he had begun to appreciate that writing was done to some purpose, and that it would influence his knowledge and decisions in life. In the very basic sense used in this book he had grasped some understanding of the act of writing. What was doubtful was the extent to which he appreciated the personal element in authorship – that text originated in someone's hand, as well as appearing in the signs and print around him. His own writing developed very slowly, in spite of initial reasonable motor skill in copying. It was as though he could see little point in much that was required, though number work writing seemed to appeal more. It was quite possible that here he was intuitively aware that what he wrote actually mattered to the teacher. It is interesting that when a teacher expressed very positive interest in wanting to know what he might write, he responded with more lively interest and originality.

As to John's awareness of the English spelling system, signs of this began to emerge in his first year in the way his misreadings showed similar letter patterns to the 'target' words. These similarities extended from single letters in similar positions to patterns of two or three letters in corresponding positions, and the ability to recognise words embedded in the spelling of others. This sensitivity to spelling patterns preceded any attempt by the teacher to draw attention to them through naming letters or digraphs 'phonically', and, indeed, must have facilitated his understanding of what she was doing. His memory for frequently seen words was good, and through seeking sense in his reading, he was able to acquire a good store. This must have enabled unconscious processes of pattern comparison and analysis to go forward to such an extent that he was able to use visual information in new words to cue him into how they might sound. This cueing, together with the gist of what he was reading, enabled him to tackle new words with little, if any, explicit phonics, and so to move rapidly into fluent reading.

WILMA

From John we can now turn to Wilma, who also made good progress with her reading, but not with John's flair.

At 5 she was a healthy, happy child with a serious and calm disposition. Her school attendance was very good, and she showed no defects of vision or hearing. She was one of the physically more mature children for her age, being quite tall and fairly well built. Her curly dark hair, facial features and skin colour revealed a mixed racial parentage. The language of her home was, however, English

– and local dialect English at that, for she spoke like the other children of the area. She had an older sister, and lived with her mother who was a trouser machinist. Her father visited, but did not live at home. A further child was born to her mother when Wilma was 6. Wilma settled very well into school in the sense that she seemed to observe and grasp what was going on and suited her behaviour to the teacher's requirements. She made friends easily, seemed happy with all her teachers, and made good progress with most of her activities in school, including reading. She reported that she received help in this respect at home, in that her mother read stories to her and to her sister, that she herself tried to read aloud to her mother and grandmother, and that she had story-books and comics at home. Her comments on her experience at home were consistent over the two years of the study, but it was not possible to obtain a report from her mother, and the accuracy could therefore not be confirmed. Nor could any account be obtained of her experience before attending school.

Once at school, however, she showed some understanding of reading, both in her references to activities at home and in her comments and behaviour in school. Early in the first term of observation she defined reading as *reading a story-book* and *learning letters*. She had observed, and she understood, something of the use of numbers and destinations on buses and of signs on shops. She realised that such signs had a purpose beyond that of decoration. She also spoke of her mother writing letters and of making shopping lists. Later that term she claimed to be able to read, but also knew that she had much to learn. She wanted to learn to read the Gay Way Red Book and was able to report the content of what she had so far read in it. She also told of the stories of Cinderella and Snow White which were in books at home. Her understanding seemed to be that books enabled readers to discover stories, but there was no hint that she thought at all of a possible author. There was an interesting difference between her understanding of writing as an intentional act of communication in the everyday world and her appreciation of text as something given in books.

Her understanding of reading and of writing seemed to be brought closer through her Breakthrough work. Unlike John she was not deterred by copying sentences she had built with the cards. She developed a careful and tidy hand, and was willing to try to write her ideas directly and to use her folder materials. On one occasion in this term she wrote *I see the dog* from memory as *I see thu dog*. She then produced a Breakthrough card version and compared them, identifying her own error. This was an example of careful attention to detail which was characteristic of her work, but which had been alien to John. As time went on, however, and she began to write more sentences freely, she gained speed in writing at the expense of neatness. Accuracy, however, was maintained, and spelling errors were not frequent as long as she remained within her Breakthrough and Gay Way vocabulary range. During her second year her free writing ventured beyond this, but was limited to a few sentences at any one time. She said at the end of that year that she had never thought of trying to write a story herself. It was not until the end of her third year, when she was 7, that she moved into really fluent reading and more extensive writing. By this time she had begun to enjoy writing in much the same spirit as she enjoyed art and music – as a medium of personal expression.

Like John she was not handicapped by a lack of understanding of reading and writing, but unlike him she had not pressed for knowledge from home or school. It seemed that her mother had wanted her to learn to read and had helped her, and that Wilma had actively responded to what was offered. The two children had different temperaments, different approaches to discovering knowledge and somewhat different understandings of the nature and purpose of literacy. Thus they both coped well with the school curriculum but with their own emphases.

Nor was Wilma handicapped by any language difficulty. At 5 she had an average command of spoken vocabulary and of syntax; she could tell a short story; she spoke easily and sensibly with teachers; and she appeared to understand their requirements and instructions. Like John she spoke with a marked local dialect, but rather than inhibiting her work in school, this seemed adequate to support her reading and to allow modification in certain contexts towards the language of textbooks and teachers.

Wilma probably started school with less exposure to English spelling than John, but she soon gained experience of words. As early as the beginning of February she could recognise and pick out seven or eight words from the Breakthrough array on the classroom wall. In Test A2 (Appendix A) in February she was able to recognise and name the letters *m*, *a*, and *c*, and the numbers 2, 3, 4 and 8. Her only errors were to deny that *t* was a letter and to be unable to name it. She seemed to distinguish clearly between the two categories of sign. In Test A3 (Appendix A), she was able to provide correctly one example of a letter (phonic), two of words and one of a sentence. She incorrectly gave a word as a further example of a sentence. She recognised two examples each of letters (phonic) and sentences but was confused about words. She could read four words in the test material. She was showing, therefore, some grasp of the terms *letter* and *sentence*, but was not sure of *word*.

Observation of her work in class towards the end of February revealed that she had compiled a personal 'reading book' which contained sentences she could build and read using the Breakthrough scheme. From initial sentence-frames of *I see a*. . . she had widened her ability with frames *I am*. . ., *I go to*. . . and *I like*. . . . When reading them all she commented with a suggestion of boredom, 'There's too many *I*'s', apparently meaning there were a lot. They were also salient, taking the initial position in all cases. When asked to make a new sentence from her folder of words (at this stage containing thirty-two Breakthrough words and twelve others added by Wilma) she first said the sentence and then built it, in this way compiling *I go to school from home* and *I like baking*. These may well have occurred in general teaching sessions with the class, but now she was making them her own. She was able to copy them reasonably well. Shortly after this she was introduced to the Gay Way scheme, adding new words to her Breakthrough folder as she met them. She also had a specially constructed reading book made by the teacher to introduce the actual Gay Way Red Book. She was beginning to read the latter, and her errors were particularly interesting. Taking the first three pages she read the first sentence correctly but made mistakes with the others. She could not read *in* in the phrase *went up the hill in the lorry* and made no attempt to guess. She confused *pots* and *pans* and even with guidance drawing attention to the *o/a* difference (she could name and draw these letters on request) she still had difficulty. She stalled at capital letters in *The* (except the first sentence), *Big* and *Red*, failing to read these words although she read *the*, *big* and *red* correctly in more than one context. Overall she gave the impression of adopting the strategy of learning items thoroughly, and not guessing.

By mid-March when interviewed according to schedule A4 (Appendix A) she was ready to claim that she could read, obviously feeling some mastery of the skill. Her reported purpose in learning was to read the Red Book. In talking about this she said she found it hard when she did not know some of the words. Her reading revealed a good memory store of the words involved, but no way of attacking a new or forgotten word. When asked how she knew what the page said she replied that she used her eyes and did not need glasses. When she did not know a word she would ask the teacher. She did not think that pictures helped her. Again, then, she seemed to depend on accurate visual memory, gleaning meaning from what she read rather than reading according to some guessed meaning.

When asked for a word that she found hard she offered *lorry* – a surprise in that she always seemed to read it correctly. She gave two reasons for finding it hard – it was a bit like *down* and a bit like *little*.

Perhaps then Wilma was sorting out graphic similarities that could lead to error, in the above cases a second position *o* and a first position *l*. She was not simply remembering visual forms. She was able to identify some similarities and differences very readily – now having no difficulty with *pots* and *pans*; being able to deny any similarity between *down* and *have*; but seeing the corresponding *h*, *o* and *e* letters in *house* and *home* and the absence or presence of *m*. Her dependence on learned sentence-frames was shown in a very simple task. She constructed and read *I am a boy* in response to a request to make a sentence. When the words were rearranged to *am I a boy* she read it correctly but denied that it was a sentence, giving the reason '*I* should be first'. (This also seemed to be a rule of John's.) The further rearranged array *boy am a I* was also read correctly, and she gave the same reason for rejecting it as a sentence. Given a less familiar frame *Ben is a dog* she was able to read it successfully, to allow it to be a sentence and also to read the question version and allow it also to be a sentence. She rejected the nonsense array *Ben dog a is*. It was possibly the case, then, that an early dependence on a restricted frame interfered with specific examples for a time, although greater flexibility was being shown with new frames. It is worth noting that she commented on the *I*s in her first personal sentence-book. She was responding to pattern in both sentences and words.

The second term ended in mid-April when the children were tested with a word list and a few sentences culled from the Breakthrough materials (see Appendix A, Test A5), which formed the backbone of the class reading activities at that stage. Wilma read twenty-one of the thirty words, made no attempt at *television*, *like*, *birthday*, *good*, *baby* and *my*, and misread *home* as *house*, *he* as *hen*, and *are* as *red*. The spelling similarities are obvious. She nevertheless read *television* correctly in two of the sentences but not in a third. The other two omitted words which occurred in the sentences, *like* and *my*, were managed less well. Yet earlier she had read all three words correctly in her personal book. The mistake with *television* was interesting. After reading *I see a television* correctly, Wilma stalled with *I like television*. She did not read *like* and, having omitted it, read *baking* for television. Now a sentence in her own personal booklet was *I like baking*, and one was left with the impression that *like* triggered the word *baking*, and the common *k* caused confusion. But not liking to read *I baking* ——, she settled for making *baking* the final word. *My* was confused with *made*, for Wilma read *I can see made television*, and yet when she encountered *I like my dogs* she read *like* as *made* and this seemed to release in her the chance to read *my* correctly for she read *I made my dogs*. The spelling similarities led to confusion, but some awareness of appropriacy of words following *I* seemed also to be involved. In no case did she show any sign of attempting to sound a word.

The same test was given to the children in the third term in June. Wilma read twenty-four words correctly this time. *Good*, *baby* and *birthday* were still not known, *television*, *home* and *my* were read correctly but *are* and *he* were not attempted. *Like* still caused trouble and was also not read. There were no misreadings. But by now she was adopting a further strategy. When faced with a new word which might before have been misread on a basis of spelling similarity, she now attempted a phonic attack. She appeared to have forgotten *big*, *at*, *it* and *bed* which she read correctly in April (but note the confusion possibilities if only partly learned or forgotten), and a phonic attack led to successful reading. She was obviously encouraged and excited by the successful outcomes, but puzzled by the unsuccessful. Given that she had successfully jumped from *h o m e* (sounded separately and phonetically) to *home* (sounded correctly) one supposed that this related to seeking a cue that distinguished *house* and *home*. If so, then the silent *e* rule was not used. After completing the test she was therefore led back to *home* and the silent *e* and vowel change were explained to her. Then she was asked to try *like* again and she readily applied the rule after first sounding the letters individually with the *e* non-silent. She was delighted, and seemed to be encouraged to think that 'sounding' still had a future.

Although she had brought phonic analysis into her repertoire her graphic analytic skills were also developing further. Given the task of finding words 'hiding' in others she was able to see *dog* in *dogs*, *cat* in *cats*, *pin* and *in* in *pink*, *red* in *tired* and *rib* in *redistribute*.

Also in June she read a booklet prepared for use with all children who had started the Gay Way Red Book. She read most of the familiar book sentences very well but failed completely with *A tin pot fell down*. She had trouble with both *A* which she read as *And*, and *tin* which she could not recall and for which, interestingly enough, she did not try a phonic attack. Perhaps this early material was not associated in her memory with her more recent phonic strategies. In no context did she read *tin* correctly, though in one word list she read it as *the* and in the other as *in*. Graphic similarities were obviously involved. In other sentences, too, she read *And* for *A*. That these difficulties inhibited her reading of the later part of the sentence was suggested by the otherwise correct readings of *pot*, *fell* and *down* in other contexts, including other sentences in the booklet. More errors were made in unfamiliar sentences constructed from the same words and phrases as the familiar, suggesting that sentence familiarity was adding to Wilma's reading, but this was only marginally so. Indeed, she read word lists almost as accurately as familiar sentences, and the novel sentences only slightly less well. It was the novel sentences which yielded most error, suggesting interference with established patterns of recall. This, however, would imply that although Wilma's prime strategy was to use visual memory and visual analysis of the written code, she was nevertheless aware of sentence relationships.

In July, when she had progressed in the Gay Way scheme to the Blue Book, a further sample of her reading was recorded. She read less fluently than in the earlier book, for she now had to attack new words more frequently and could depend less on word memory. In the following transcripts the hyphenating indicates a phonic attack, and an asterisk shows that help was required. Brackets enclose self-corrected misreadings.

> I c-u-t, cut up the old s-a-c-k, sack with my scissors, and you p-u-t, put the b-i-t-s, bits in you*, your nest. But I did not take the eggs (out) a-w-a-y, away*. So then the (red in) r-o-d-i-n, r-o-b-i-n robin went to K-e-n, Ken, the little boy with the s-t-i-c-k, stick*. O-p-e-n, open* the window, Ken. Did you take my (six eggs out) eggs a-w-a-y, away*? I lost six o-u-t, out* of my nest t-o-d-a-y, today*. (age 5 years 4 months)

The self-correction is interesting in that the first reading tends to be a carry-over from some previous reading, which is then *seen* not to be right. It is semantically and syntactically appropriate following what has gone before, so that only visual information can be the basis of correction. In one instance only is the later part of the sentence such that the error could not easily be squared with sense. The phonic attack is successful with simple grapheme–phoneme correspondence but not with the more complex patterns. When help was given *your* was solved by asking for a similar word which was supplied by Wilma as *you*. When she then tried to read *your* she seemed suddenly to slip from *you* to *your* as the appropriate word in the phrase *in your nest*. Thus a phonic analysis was not attempted. With *stick* the information that *ck* generally made the single sound was enough, while with *Open* the information about vowel sound was given simply for that word as it stood. For *today* and *away* the task was more difficult. The *ay* aspect was not resolved by drawing attention to the sound or to its occurrence in both words. It was only sounded as specific to each, but tended to break down if the first part of the word was not solved. Finally the solution which Wilma found most helpful was to break each word into two before combining them, as *a* plus *way* and *to* plus *day*. She was quite able to accept the associated variation of meanings. This finding was consistent with the previous observation that her visual analytic skills were more 'advanced' than her phonic.

In a later interview with John, when both children attempted to read from the Second Blue Book, Wilma again worked hard with new words. When asked which she found particularly hard and why, she reported that she found *shoe* difficult because it looked like *sand* and *school* and did not sound properly. *Inside* was hard because it had *in* and *side*, and *new* because it 'looked hard'. Lest it be thought that her concentration on accuracy and analysis prevented her understanding, it should be said that she could always show good comprehension of what she had read when questioned with the book closed, and she was often aware when misreadings did not fit the scheme of things. But she did not appear to be willing to offer a reading based only or almost only on expectations from meaning. She read aloud when both meaning *and* visual information gave her sufficient confidence in her reading.

In all, Wilma's careful approach to her reading, her patient, thorough learning, her development of orthographic knowledge and her attempts to 'sound' without too much discouragement in the face of puzzlement had characterised her work all year. They lay behind her steady progress through the reading scheme which made her the best girl reader in the class, and possibly, at this stage, a better reader than John.

Early in her second year she used her careful visual analytic skills to good effect in Test B2 (Appendix B). She easily sorted big and little words, and matched simple letters very quickly. In this second item she did more than she was asked, volunteering the matching of *sh* in *ship* and *sheep* and giving the sound of the pair. She also noticed the similarity of the final *p*. She was very quick to respond in all the items, matching initial-, final- and central-letter patterns very well. Even the three-letter final patterns were readily seen. Her oral sentence completion was very good.

Wilma's work in class at this stage included writing in a sentence-book into which she copied sentences she had constructed with her sentence-maker and had checked with the teacher. She was obviously able to construct freely within the vocabulary constraints, and her sentence-maker contained 105 items including the elements *ed*, *ing*, *s*, *?* and the full stop. Her ventures into sentence construction had led the teacher to supply these bound morphemes and punctuation marks. In this booklet, as in her number work booklet, her handwriting was clear and steady when she was copying a model.

Her free writing in her number-book was less steady, but still correct and legible.

In a repetition of the Breakthrough Test A5 (Appendix A) she improved little on her performance of about six months previously, but read a slightly different selection of words. One or two of her misreadings, where she attempted a phonic approach to a non-regular word, were quite at sea. This gave food for thought, for, in spite of her initial careful learning and her obvious ability to recognise visual pattern in words, she was not able to manage as well as John, who had seemed to give less care to his learning and less detailed attention to text. Moreover, she had tried to use phonics more than he had. The translation of visual information through some sufficient level of knowledge of orthography to smooth oral reading is clearly both highly skilful and below the level of awareness. Is it possible that a child can attend to detail too much for comfort?

In early November Wilma's reading from her current reader, the Third Blue Book, was sampled. This text was obviously presenting her with more problems than the Red Book series had done. (In order to encourage fluent reading the teacher was also requiring her to read from supplementary easier books.) The following gives a transcript of her reading.

Extract from the Third Blue Book (Gay Way)
He sleeps and eats and sleeps and eats all day long.
What do you think he likes to eat?
He likes to eat things that are four years old.

Wilma's reading to observer (Age 5 years 8 months)
W: He slept and he slept and he . . . I've got it wrong! He slept . . .
O: Try it again. Can you sound it?
W: s-l-e-e-p-s, sleeps (confidently)
O: Good girl.
W: sleeps and he sl . . . e-a-t-s, eats (confidently)
O: Good girl.
W: and sleeps and eats all (pronounced as in *pal* and felt to be wrong) a-l, along . . .
O: No, that was a good guess but not quite right.
W: all b, d-a-y . . .
O: Try *d-ay*.
W: day long. W-h-a-t . . . h-a-t makes hat, but I don't know what that sound is.
O: You have to remember it's *what*.

W: What do you want . . .
O: Try again.
W: t-h-i-n-k . . . that makes *hin* (pointing to middle three letters) and that makes *tin* (pointing to the first, third and fourth).
O: *t* and *h* together make *th*.
W: th-i-n . . . think he likes to eat. He likes to eat the grass . . .
O: Remember *t* and *h* make *th*.
W: thinks . . .
O: Not a *k*, is it?
W: grass (hesitatingly) . . .
O: Try again carefully.
W: things out of . . .
O: Try to sound it.
W: th-a-t, that ran . . .
O: (recapitulating) He likes to eat the things that . . .
W: are from . . .
O: Try again. This is hard, but you're doing nicely.
W: f-o-u-r . . . There's lots of new words in this book.
O: Yes. That one's *four*.
W: four y-e-a-r-s . . .
O: years.
W: o-l-d . . . lot . . .
O: say *oh* for *o, old*.
W: old.
O: Now can you read it all again to see if you've got it?
W: He sleeps and he eats and he sleeps and he eats (lots) all day long. What do you think he likes to eat? He likes to eat the things that are four years old.
   (This last was read fairly smoothly, with intonation, but contained the unnoticed extra *he* and the corrected extra *lots*.)

Given the number of checks to get words right it seemed possible that Wilma was losing sight of all meaning, but two indications that this was not so were the fluent re-reading she managed at the end, and the 'meaningful' errors made at the first attempt. Thus while the work seemed hard for her, it did not defeat her, and her own reaction amounted to 'That's hard, but I like it!' It was clear that she was operating at both graphic and phonic levels of decoding and that both presented problems. Her misreading of *sleeps* came home to her, the error presumably being along the lines of incomplete graphic pattern recognition, but her phonic skills enabled her to tackle the word successfully from a different angle. Sometimes neither graphic nor phonic attacks helped because neither the grapheme pattern nor the phoneme pattern was yet known; and if semantic predictability from the text was virtually nil, then help was needed. The form of help was a matter for the observer's judgement, for it was clear that there were options. The thorny question of how best to help to tune in with the child's strategies raised its head. Here nothing can be offered to justify the decisions made, for they were intuitive rather than planned. The moves adopted at least satisfied the criterion that Wilma was able to use them, but whether they were the best in terms of her needs at that time could not be judged without an elusive spelling out of her requirements. Given that John also read the same text, it is instructive to compare the two transcripts. He seemed to depend very little on explicit sounding and to be able to extend his earlier skill more readily into this new material.

By mid-November Wilma was accumulating written work in her number- and writing-books. Her copying was now very similar to her free writing, both virtually error-free but somewhat erratic in line. It was doubtful whether she now actually copied carefully, she seemed rather to identify the model letter or word and then write it freely. She could read all that she had written, and could interpret and use addition and equal signs in simple numerical addition problems. Her writing-book included individual original sentences, but not yet any sequence forming some kind of story or description.

In early December her reading was sampled again. She was still using the Third Blue Book and reading from 'The Lazy, Hungry Crocodile'. She tended to read one word at a time, but with more fluency and intonation than in her reading from the same book a month earlier.

Extract from the Third Blue Book (Gay Way)
Next day he woke up and said, I am a very hungry crocodile. I am getting so thin. I must get my dinner, my four-year-old dinner. So he came out of the mud to look for his dinner. Jip the cat sat under a tree.

Wilma's reading (Age 5 years 9 months)
Next (door) day he woke up and said, I am a v-e-r-y, very hungry crocodile. I am g-e-t-t-i-n-g . . . that's *tin* and that's *ing* . . . getting s . . . so t-h-i-n, thin*. I must get (me) my dinner, my four-year-old dinner. So he came out of the mud to look for his dinner.
Jip the cat sat u . . . u-n-d . . . under (the) a tree.

Unlike the previous occasion help was only called for once – with *thin*, where the unvoiced *th* was offered instead of Wilma's voiced version. All the corrections were made by Wilma herself immediately after the error, and all sounding was self-initiated and successfully completed. She was reading very carefully, and managed without hesitation words she had only recently found difficult. Moreover, she volunteered information about her reactions to the text when she commented, as an intermediate step between sounding the individual letters and pronouncing the full word, that *tin* and *ing* were in *getting*. She seemed to be combining letter pattern perception with sounding at something approaching a syllabic level.

The following sample of her reading was made towards the end of March, by which time she was 6.

Extract from the Fourth Blue Book (Gay Way)
Then he runs all the way back again. Down the street, up the next street, over the road across the bridge, along the grass by the water and back to his house. Then he begins again. He runs and runs and runs all the way and back again.

Her reading was so fluent that a transcript is of little interest. The only points where she hesitated were to correct herself when she misread *runs* as *ran*, to sound *d-ow-n* before reading *Down*, and to correct a slightly odd rendering of *again*.

A further sampling in June is given below.

Extract from the Fifth Blue Book (Gay Way)
One day Pip came out of school and ran down the street to her house. She went in at the gate and up three steps. She ran into the kitchen to see Jip and the kitten. And what did she see? The kitten was standing up in the basket. He began to walk round and round the basket. He walked round his mother. He tried to walk on her slippery fur. But his little paws slipped and he tumbled. Jip gave him a lick and he began to walk again round and round the basket. Then he lay down and went to sleep.

Wilma's reading (Age 6 years 3 months)
One day Pip came out of school and ran down the street to her house. She went in at the gate and up (street . . . tree . . . t-h-r-e-e . . . through . . .) three* steps. She ran into the kitchen to see Jip and (her) the kitten. And what did she see? The kitten was s-t-a . . . standing up in the basket. He b-e-g-a-n, began to walk round and round the basket. He walked round his mother. He (t-r-i . . . tripped . . . t-r-i-e-d) tried to walk on her s-l-i-p-p-e-

r-y, slip . . . slippery* fur. But his little p-a-w-s paw-s, paws slip-p-e-d, slipped* and he (turned . . . tippled . . .) t-u-m-b-l-e-d, tumbled. Jip gave him a l-i-c-k, lick and he be-gan, began to walk a-g-a-i-n, again round and round the b-a-s-k-e-t, basket*. Then he lay down and went to sleep.

Wilma read fluently for some sentences, but word by word for others. She was successful with sounding except for the four aster-isked words for which she needed a final prompt. The misreadings of *three* given as *street* and *tree* were interesting for their graphic similarity, as was the help needed with the *ee* after 'sounding' had broken it up.

By the end of this second year in school she was conscious that John was outpacing her, and her morale was quite seriously affected. The two children had set up a friendly 'race' during their first year and could clearly judge each other's performance. Her third year began with Wilma feeling somewhat downcast, and still stumbling over some of her reading.

In November of her third year in school she read the following extract from the Seventh Blue Book.

Extract from 'The Greedy Grey Wolf' (Age 6 years 8 months)
One day (a) the red fox met (a) the (greedy) grey wolf.
'Red Fox,' said (greedy) Grey Wolf, 'Will you let me come and live with you? I will (chopped) chop the st-i-ck-s, sticks for the fire. I will wash up. I will make the beds and sweep the floor.'
'And what do you (wa-) want me to do?' said Red Fox.
'You will go out (to) and get the dinner,' said the grey wolf.
The fox did not know that the wolf was very greedy. He liked to eat all day long.
So the fox said, 'Yes, you can come and live with me.' Then he took the wolf into his house.
'Chop the sticks and sweep the house,' he said, '(I w . . . wa . . .) I want to go to sleep.'
Grey Wolf (d . . ., b-g- . . ., bepped, beg . . .) began to chop the sticks and (swept, sweept, swept) sweep the house.

Wilma read rather slowly and a little jerkily, but in phrases rather than words. She did not need assistance when she came to a difficulty, and seemed to use sounding to gain clues rather than to seek a solution to finding a word. The earlier corrections in the passage were made in response to the observer's indication that more attention was needed, and were made rapidly. The errors were syntactically and semantically appropriate and suggested anticipatory reading rather than the dependence on recall which had previously marked her reading. As a matter of interest, she was asked to read a further part of the story silently. She read on in a very quiet whisper, so she was then asked to read without any noise at all. She then read with accompanying lip movements. Her comprehension when reading like this was just as good as when reading aloud.

When seen in class, working from the same Sound Sense booklet as John, she was well able to cope with the exercises. Her handwriting was not fluent, but words were clearly spaced and of a good size. She was absent for Test C2 (Appendix C), but tackled C3 very sensibly. Like John she firmly put words with non-English orthography in a 'foreign' pile, but within English orthography she judged three true and most nonsense words to be non-English, and two nonsense words to be true words. There appeared to be some misreading, possibly due to the lack of sentence support which normally helped her to decide on words for which she had graphic or phonic cues. She did not attempt any overt sounding or evident sub-vocalisation, although her previous reading had suggested that she might. In the *e*-cancellation task she was typically careful, so much so that of the children concerned she deleted by far the greatest number. The only letters missed were all non-sounded *e*s in the final position, and she deleted only half of these. The *e*-cancelling hypothesis of detecting sensitivity to phonics seemed to hold for her, but interpreting such a finding was tricky. In the light of all the information gleaned about her reading, it seemed likely that the finding might indicate sub-vocalisation while doing the task but not necessarily any particular phonic analytic skill.

In February Wilma read the following.

Extract from the Yellow Book (Gay Way) (age 6 years 11 months)
'I will swim on the p-ond, pond,' said the duck.
'I will jump in (the) and h-i-d-e, hide* on the armchair,' s-p-e-a-k-ed, squeaked* the pin.
'I will jump in (the) and lie down on the bed,' squeaked the needle.
'I will get up on the window-sill,' said the stone.
Then Mr Badman came home. He went in (the) and be-g-a-n, began to blow up the fire. But the cat rushed at him and scratched dust all over him.

Here Wilma only required help with the asterisked words. Elsewhere she corrected herself or discovered the word through phonic clues quite spontaneously. Where she needed help simple phonics would not do, and the cues she did obtain were not sufficiently supported by expected meanings to be of much use. That she did not manage *hide* was interesting in the light of the *e*-cancellation finding and seemed to support the interpretation given.

Given that Wilma had made such a promising start with her reading, but had plodded through her third year while John had leapt ahead, it was thought that the Daniels and Diack tests might be helpful in pinpointing her difficulties. In the basic reading test she did very well with the simple single questions, but stalled at the multiple choice question-and-answer items. She appeared to be outfaced by their apparent complexity and would not attempt questions and phrases she could reasonably be expected to read at least in part. This seemed to be a cognitive block, linked with her reluctance to guess. She did not quite do well enough to justify giving her the silent prose reading test if the test manual recommendations were to be followed, but she enjoyed reading the passage concerned and answered the comprehension questions well. It seemed reasonable to stay with the hypothesis that the slowing down of Wilma's progress was linked with a reluctance to take anticipatory risks with reading materials.

The copying task was also revealing. In spite of her earlier success with simple copy tasks and letter pattern recognition, she failed in this more complex copying to achieve either good accuracy or neatness. This could be linked with her apparent difficulty in extending her skill with pattern recognition to the more generalised fluent knowledge of orthography which could be associated with fluent reading. While John seemed to be inclined to overshoot detail, Wilma seemed slow to generalise or contextualise it.

She was also successful with the simpler diagnostic word recognition test, but began to find difficulty when moving from single-syllable to polysyllabic words. She was able to sound letters and to blend consonants, but could not synthesise some double syllables. Even when successful she tended to be slow. She also had difficulty with the words requiring further phonic rules for vowels and their combinations with other letters such as *r*, and made one or two letter position and reversal errors. Nevertheless her performance on the word recognition tasks 8 and 9 indicated no fundamental problem in associating visual and aural analysis. What the tests had highlighted were her over-cautious approach and a limitation on complexity of information processing. Further maturity, practice and experience might be expected to see continued progress.

By June of that year some of this improvement was already evident. She read an extract from the Second Violet Book fluently, with ease, and with very good intonation. Her teacher reported that she was regaining her confidence, that she was beginning to write more than a sentence or two at a time, and that she was enjoying writing. Her reading and writing were good enough to support wider curriculum work, and she was proving to be more artistic and musical than many of her classmates.

SUMMARY

These case studies have been spelled out in some detail to illustrate the basis for the following conclusions. Both children effectively began to read during their first year in school, not having tried to learn more than some 'environment word' recognition at home, nor being pressed to do so. They had both learned enough about the act of reading, however, to be able to respond to school instruction, and from time to time they received support at home during their school years. This took the form of access to suitable materials, listening to an adult reading, and trying to read to an adult. The last, the active attempt to read not just to listen, seemed very important. Both children were able to take part in the kind of dialogue which is the basis for learning, being able to question, explain and consider alternatives and to give some thematic account of events. Their strong local dialect did not interfere with their understanding of the speech of their teachers, or of the text of their books. Indeed, their reading aloud showed some adaptation of their speech towards the form of the teacher's reading of the text.

During their first year they gained a clear understanding of reference to letters, words and sentences in text and, from the beginning, understood that their own spoken sentences could be represented in print. They were thus not only learning to associate spoken with written words, but also to refer to and attend to the detailed technicalities of the relationship. This meant they were able to acquire the sort of knowledge that allowed them in their second year to 'take off' into reading and constructing written sentences they had not previously encountered.

Before they were able to make such progress they showed some interesting early learning. Their initial strength lay in becoming very familiar with a restricted pool of words and a very limited set of sentence-frames. Their expectations about sentences showed they realised that word order was important, but that they thought rearrangements of familiar sentences were not part of the game. Each sentence was a separate package to be learned in its own right. Words, and letter order, were similarly treated at first. But both children rapidly moved into a recognition of more general word patterning across sentences and of letter patterning across words. In doing so they showed ability to respond to cues from meaning and spelling as long as they were operating within the scope of materials such as their Breakthrough folders or their first Gay Way readers, where much new reading was based on a rearrangement of words already encountered. Thus phrases would lead to expected next words, and visual cues from these next words would trigger memory of a limited set of words from which to select. The combined effect was likely to yield success, and all the time the cues were being associated with the phonetic forms of the words as read aloud. The outcome of this early learning was a growth of knowledge of English spelling and a move towards more challenging reading materials.

The challenge was to come when the pool of words to be read expanded well beyond the small, familiar, early set. This was when they moved away from the Gay Way Red Book series. At this point individual strategies, which had been shown to some extent earlier, became more evident. John leaned heavily on predicting new words from the sense of what he was reading, and on checking them from visual cues and the sense of what followed. He did not seem to need to attend to all the letters in most words. Wilma tried to identify each new word completely and accurately, rather than taking too much of a risk with meaning. She therefore attempted to make more use of the phonic strategies she had been taught. Before this both children had responded to early phonics teaching by learning to name letters phonically, which aided letter recognition, and to build 'regular' simple words from phonic analysis to letter patterns; but they had used phonics very little in actual reading, finding that the visual pattern, together with meaning and saying the whole word, met their needs. When they tried to use phonics in the face of more challenging text they met irregularities or obscure regularities of correspondence of sound with letter, which daunted them. John seemed able to by-pass the problem by explicitly using phonics only enough to give him sufficient sound to add to the sense and visual cues and so resolve his uncertainty. It took Wilma much longer to get to this point. One was reminded of children learning to swim. John was like the youngster who has confidence to strike out without too much refinement of technique, and who improves his strokes as he swims. Wilma was like the child who works at arm and leg strokes in the shallow end, but eventually has to take to the water to 'put it all together' in real swimming.

Chapter 5

The Slower Learners

Of the remaining eight children Mary, Sean and Dave made more significant progress than the others, though Dave's reading score was almost two years behind the norm by the end of his third year in school. All three attended school regularly, and had no identified defects of vision or hearing. They scored above the norm on the English Picture Vocabulary test at 7, and their general behaviour and conversation suggested no particular learning difficulties, but they were slow to learn to read. Although there was some suggestion of support at home, it was not strong. Neither the children nor their parents appeared to mind the leisurely pace, and there seemed to be no enthusiasm on either side beyond a mild interest. At times, in fact, all three children expressed some disinclination or lack of interest. Their approach to reading will be described in the order of their ability at 7, Mary having made most progress and being followed by Sean and Dave.

MARY

Mary was rather a quiet, diffident 5-year-old when she entered school, but sometimes she became boisterous in her play with others. She gained confidence during the year as she found what was expected of her and as she became accustomed to life in the classroom group. By her second year she had made friends but was still somewhat quiet. She was rather slight in build, but her health seemed fairly robust. She was the youngest of five children, with two brothers and two sisters. Her father was a conductor/driver with the city transport service and her mother was a clerical worker. She made good initial progress with learning to read and reported that she received various kinds of help at home. This was confirmed by her mother at an interview when Mary was 6. Her mother said that she talked about her school reading and about stories and other activities. She could read street signs and bus numbers before she went to school. She had a few books of her own at home, and her mother anticipated that she would soon be able to read some of the religious tracts which her parents valued highly. She had asked her mother to read to her even before she went to school, and her mother had done so; and when Mary was at school she had also listened to her trying to read. She had a realistic view of her ability at 6½, expecting the Gay Way Blue Book to be appropriate but a little bit hard. She knew Mary could write her name and some short sentences. The overall picture given by her mother was one of a helpful home in terms of learning to read, though with a possibly somewhat restricted outlook in relation to later reading.

Yet on entering school Mary, like John, had to learn the introductory Breakthrough words. Her comments about reading suggested that she equated it with learning to read rather than with reading in everyday life, but she did report that her mother read a story 'about Toby' to her, and that both parents read the newspaper. Later that term, after making good progress with the Breakthrough materials, she thought that she herself could read, but that she would read harder books later. She had started to read the Gay Way Red Book by then, and claimed that she found the pictures helped her to read. It seemed they functioned as cues to help her recall words and sentences she had already come across. She saw reading as the recall of recent learning, not the tackling of new words. If she did not know a word she would ask the teacher or she would 'think', by which she seemed to mean that she would try to see if she could remember it. In this she was like Wilma, and her early progress was very similar.

She also had some idea of writing, possibly as an act of authorship. She had been taught at home to write her name and she could copy a sentence accurately. Unlike Wilma and John she could almost write a sentence, both dictated and original, as well as being able to suggest original sentences to be constructed with Breakthrough materials. A feature of her classwork was her ability to read the sentences she had stored in her personal writing-book, and these were as complicated as *I like my house because it has beautiful windows*. Few, if any, of the other children in the class could do this – most who could copy their Breakthrough sentences could not re-read them accurately on a later occasion. Throughout her first year in school Mary showed more interest in writing than in reading, and by the end of her first year was more successful at writing dictated and original sentences than any of the other children in the sample of ten. Yet improvement during her second year was slow, leaving her reading age lagging behind her vocabulary and chronological ages at 7. For some reason her interest in reading seemed low. Yet her understanding of the nature of reading and writing and of their various uses seemed more than adequate. It was in the middle of her third year in school that she began to be more enthusiastic, and her reading became more fluent, but at this point her family moved and she went to another school. A postscript to her story was obtained from the headmistress of the school to which she moved, and this spoke of the problems she faced in finding her feet again in new surroundings which included a different reading scheme and a greater emphasis on phonics. She had not responded readily to this and had not appeared to progress much at first, but after six months or so was beginning to read better and to produce interesting free writing. She still preferred writing to reading, and it seemed possible that she might have learned to read more quickly through learning to write rather than constructing sentences from ready-made printed Breakthrough words, for such an approach *for her* would have tapped more interest, and might well have led her to give greater attention to remembering how words were constructed.

Certainly no deficit in spoken language appeared to interfere with her learning. Her English Picture Vocabulary test score was comfortably above the norm and, although somewhat reserved, she showed no problems in talking with and understanding her teachers. She enjoyed retelling a story when she was 6, and produced a coherent account. Like John's and Wilma's her retelling included signs of some shift from her usual dialect towards 'text' English. For example, she consistently used *he was* where in speech she would have said *he were*. She also enjoyed the tests designed to explore language use in various tasks, showing effective use in explanation, supposition and reporting.

Her knowledge of the spelling of English is best reviewed in the context of her initially good, but later slower, progress in reading.

Her early progress led to Mary's having a personal writing-book containing fourteen different sentences based on her Breakthrough sentence-maker work by the middle of her second term in school. For the most part she was able to read them, but relied entirely on memory and context, for she had no way of tackling words she had forgotten. But context had to be interpreted not only as sentence meaning but also as sentence-frame. In other words, as has already been suggested for John and Wilma, she had some expectations about the structure of written sentences. The following summary of her reading (omissions bracketed) of the sentences shows how strongly a sense of frame might operate. An adequate memory would distinguish the whole of the one and only sentence not beginning with *I* on that basis alone. On the other hand, discrimination between similar frames required the correct reading of words such as *dog* and *cat*, and *see* and *love*.

I see a television.
I see a (baby).
I see my dog.
I see my cat.
I see (my) television.
I am Mary.
My mum does a lot of work.
I see a (house).
I played (out) in the snow.
I (play with) my doll.
I (like doing PE).
I love my dog.
I love my cat.
I am a good girl.

It was interesting that she did not read *my* in the second *television* sentence. It was the only instance of *my* which could be confused with *a* in an otherwise identical context. Here we have evidence of pattern perception across sentences. What of pattern across words?

She did not appear very sure of the term *word* in Test A3 (Appendix A), being more confident when referring to *sentence*, but by the end of the term, in Test A4, she was able to respond appropriately to its use. Here she was able to judge *house* and *home* as similar, seeing the common pattern of *h*, *o* and *e*. She was also able to label letters in words in a phonic manner. Like John and Wilma she responded to scrambled sentences with expectations about sentence-frames. She was thus perceiving visual pattern at both sentence and word levels. The latter began to show more clearly in her misreadings towards the end of the year. In the Breakthrough test she misread *can* as *cat*, *boy* as *baby*, *baby* as *bed*, *we* as *went*, and *are* as *red*. This was in one sense a step forward from complete or no success at word recognition. Yet she was still heavily dependent on sentence context and whole word recognition in her attempts to read. She managed familiar sentences from the Gay Way book more successfully than unfamiliar ones composed of exactly the same words, even when the constituent phrases were familiar. She also made virtually no misreadings, preferring to omit words she did not recognise. These two features suggested a strong dependence on memory rather than on linguistic sensitivity at both grammatical and orthographic levels. Such errors as she made were to substitute a familiar sentence or phrase for an unfamiliar.

By the end of the year she had worked through the First and Second Red Books and was reading the Third with her teacher. The following is a transcript of her reading to the author.

Extract from the Third Red Book (Gay Way)
Jip the cat and Ben the dog sat in the tin pot house. The pot house
is old.
Can we live in a new house?
Meg the hen and Deb the rat sat in the little shoe house on the hill.
The little shoe house is old.
Can we live in a new house?

Mary's reading (Age 5 years 4 months)
Jip the cat and Ben the dog sat in the tin pot house. The (old)
(top) p-o-t, pot (is) house is old. Can we (get a new (one) house)
live in a new house? Meg the hen and Deb the rat sat in the little
(old) shoe house (in) on the hill. The little shoe house is old. Can
we live in a new house?

In spite of interruptions when Mary's attention was drawn to
her misreadings, she read with reasonable intonation and fairly
smoothly. But again she tended to substitute or add familiar words
and phrases rather than read the precise text. Two pointers to an
ability to seek more information from the text came from her
decision to try to sound *pot* and from questioning her about word
similarity. To this she was able to suggest that *shoe, can* and *the* all
had a letter in common with *sat* and that *rat* had 'two of them'. When
naming letters she did so phonically. Although she was not able to
read new or forgotten words as John and Wilma could by this stage,
she seemed to be on the verge of doing so.

Her responses to Test B2 (Appendix B) early in her second year
indicated as ready a spelling pattern recognition as Wilma's or
John's, and her Breakthrough test performance at this stage showed
misreadings with orthographic similarity, but it was rather surprising that with such 'much read' words she failed to discriminate
between them. With her Gay Way book she was willing to try
'sounding' if encouraged to do so, but was still not inclined to use it
spontaneously.

Extract from the Fourth Red Book (Gay Way)
Who will make the door? We will make the door, said the big
water rats. Bang, bang, bang, bang. The big water rats made the
door. Who will make the windows? We will make the windows,
said the fat water rats. Bang, bang, bang, bang. The fat water rats
made the windows.

Mary's reading (Age 5 years 8 months)
Who will m-a-k-e, make* the door? W-e, we will m . . . make the door, said the big w-a-t-e-r rats, water rats. Bang, bang, bang, bang. The big water rats m-a-d-e, made* the door. Who will make the windows? W-e, we will make the windows, said the (big) fat water rats. Bang, bang, bang, bang. The (big) fat water rats made the windows.

This was fairly fluent reading, but there was no spontaneous sounding nor management of silent *e*. Mary responded to encouragement to sound quite successfully, and easily managed to blend the asterisked words where she required help. It was noticeable that she had no trouble with further examples of these words in this reading. Her error with *big* for *fat* was clearly an expectancy error, carrying through from the earlier sentences, and each instance was self-corrected.

The picture was changing a little by December of that year when she was almost 6.

Extract from the Fourth Red Book (Gay Way)
Then she sat in the nest on top of old man Tod's big black hat. She sat and sat and sat. Then she said, Brown water rats, come and see. Squeak, squeak, squeak. Little brown water rats, big brown water rats, fat brown water rats, thin brown water rats, came to look in the nest. Squeak, squeak, squeak. It is an egg. It is an egg for old man Tod, said Dilly.

Mary's reading (Age 5 years 9 months)
T-h-e-n, (hen) Th-e-n*, Then she (said) s-a . . . sat in the n-e-s-t, nest on (the) top of (the) old (man's) man Tod's big black hat. She (said) s-a . . . sat and (she) sat and sat. (Nest) Then* she said, Brown (splash) water rats come and see. (Splash) Squeak*, squeak, squeak. (The little water rats*) Little brown water rats, big brown water rats, fat brown water rats, thin brown water rats, came to (see) (black) look* in the nest. Squeak, squeak, squeak. It is an egg. It is an egg for old man Tod, (she) said Dilly.

Mary was more willing to try sounding without being prompted to do so, but she needed help with *th* in *then* each time it occurred, with *Squeak*, and with *oo* in *look*. Several errors were due to expectations that were quite appropriate, as in *said* for *sat* and the addition of *the* and *she* where they did not in fact occur. The whole phrase *The little water rats* for *Little brown water rats* was an error of this kind, and in this case her attention had to be drawn to it. It seemed likely that self-correction of expectancy errors occurred when it was seen, however dimly, that the following words did not support the reading, but that it was less likely to occur when sense still obtained. Several errors also showed graphic similarity between the reading and the correct version.

But in the second term of that school year her reading showed little change.

Extract from the Fifth Red Book (Gay Way)
Who will cut the hole in the boot for the door? We are the brown children. We will cut the hole in the boot for the door. So cut, cut, cut, cut, went the brown children.

Mary's reading (Age 5 years 11 months)
(We) Who* will (make) c-u-t, cut the h-o-l-e, hole* in the boot for the d-o-o-r, door*? We (make) a-r-e, are the brown children. We will (make) c-u-t, cut the hole in the boot (of) f-o-r, for the door. So (can) c-u-t, cut, cut, cut, cut, went the brown children.

She was still depending heavily on memory of previous reading and consequently making anticipation errors, especially where there was graphic similarity between the reading and the word. She was using sounding, but virtually only when it was suggested, in spite of her success with words like *cut*, *are* and *for*. The asterisked words are those for which she needed help because sounding letter by letter did not work. In spite of moving further in the reading scheme Mary was not showing signs of further reading abilities.

Another sample of reading was obtained in May.

Extract from the Sixth Red Book (Gay Way) (Age 6 years 2 months)
The big dog, the little cat and Tod got out of the lorry. The lorry man got out too. Open the white door and go in, said the old man. The big dog, the little cat, and the lorry man and Tod went in. Hello, hello, hello, said the children. Come in, come in. Come and see the house in the boot. And they began to clap and sing. Hello, said the old woman. Sit down, old man.

This was read smoothly and with good intonation, and errors were few. Mary did not try to sound words at which she stalled until she was asked to do so. She was then successful with *began* and *clap* (for which she had guessed *play* and *skip*, both visually similar and sensible in context). She needed help, however, with *out*, *too*, *open*, *white* (for which she first read *window* – similar visually, and sensible) and *hello*, all cases where the vowel sound defeated her. She still read rather slowly, and she was not enthusiastic about it; but she was pleasantly co-operative. It was no surprise that her reading performance on standardised tests was below the norm.

The following extract is a reading made in November of her third year from the Seventh Red Book (age 6 years 8 months).

Can you get me a new boot to put on, old woman?
Then you can have the boot house, he said.
(Will you get . . .) We will get you a new boot.
Get on the pig's back and go back (of) over* the w-a-ll, wall*. We will (put) o-p-en, open the door and go (in) o-u-t, out, (white) with* Fat Pig.

Mary read slowly and made several false moves here, but some were errors of expectation of another word, and some were confusions with similar-looking words. All in all they suggested sensitivity to the meaning of what she was reading and continued slow development of orthographic knowledge. When she was asked to read the next part of the text silently Mary did so, moving her lips as she read; and she was able to retell it in her own words afterwards. She was comprehending what she read.

Moreover, although her reading was not strong, writing still interested her, and she was able to use it both in number work and in other classwork. In November she was seen to be using a Sound Sense work-book and carrying out the exercises appropriately and tidily.

When she tried sorting the words in Test C1 (Appendix C) she distinguished English and nonsense English words from non-English at a better-than-chance level, though more of the true than the nonsense were correctly classified. She did not attempt to sound any of the words, but did read some of the English words aloud correctly as she sorted. This all suggested some growing knowledge of English orthography, but it was not possible to continue this exploration with her, or to try the Daniels and Diack diagnostic tests, for she moved to a different school about this time. Nevertheless, before she went a further reading was recorded. She read the following extract from the Fifth Green Book (age 6 years 11 months).

So he said to the old woman,
Old woman, old woman, help me to pull up the very big turnip.
The old woman (held, helped, he-l-d) held on to the old (man's) man.

Then they pulled and pulled. But they (could not) couldn't pull (it) up the very big turnip.

She read this quickly, much more quickly than she had read in previous samplings, and made errors of expectation based on text meaning. She was able to correct all her misreadings herself, though she was not always aware of error at the first reading. This was a marked improvement over her earlier performance.

It was a pity that she had to change schools at this point for she seemed about to make more rapid progress. That she did in fact master another scheme and a new approach to instruction in her new school probably reflected her readiness to move forward.

SEAN

At 5 Sean appeared to be well cared for, was of sturdy build and had a ready, twinkling smile. Throughout the study he showed good health, attended school regularly and had no vision or hearing problems. He was friendly with other children and seemed to accept school fairly easily. He was the elder of two boys whose father worked for the local water authority and whose mother was not working outside the home. In his first two years at school he adapted very well to his new surroundings and made good progress. He was friendly with adults and with other children, good-tempered, cheerful, well-behaved and competent at looking after himself. Given his general level of success it was surprising that he did not find learning to read particularly easy. He reported that he had books at home and that his parents read to him, his mother doing so nearly every day, and that he tried to read to both parents. This was confirmed at an interview with his mother when Sean was 6, and it was clear that she and her husband valued schooling as a means of getting on. When shown a copy of the Gay Way Blue Book his mother was aware that he might find it a bit hard at that stage, and that he was not finding learning too easy. She was rather puzzled about this because she found him to be an active, lively boy, who was interested in most things. He liked to tell of what he had been doing in school and he was keen on 'growing things and nature', as she put it; he had started to read signs before going to school, and had asked to be read to when quite young, and in fact still did. Both parents read to him and expected him to try to read to them, having started this practice when he was ready for school. He had started to ask for books for himself at Christmas when he was 6; and he now liked to have his own book, and was intending to join a library. It had recently become clear, however, that Sean was finding the sounding of words particularly difficult, and was indicating that he preferred other activities to reading.

His understanding of the nature of reading and writing seemed no less developed than Wilma's, Mary's, or John's. He spoke of his parents reading books and newspapers, and at 5 perceived their silent reading as different from his mother's reading aloud to him. He was able to refer to the story content of books at home, though when he started school he believed that he would have to wait until he was bigger before he could try to read them, and he showed no wish to try earlier. Unlike the other children interviewed at that stage, he expected learning to read to be a demanding task. It was almost as though his insight might be a stumbling block. This ability to assess reading as an activity was reflected throughout his first three years in his interview conversation and in remarks during various observation sessions. For instance, in the A4 interview (Appendix A) he was quite firm in his judgement that he could not yet read, and he was very unsure about why he was trying to learn. He nevertheless claimed to have a Noddy book at home and some 'clown' books he would read when he was bigger. He now said that his mother read to him nearly every day when he was in bed, and that his father sometimes read to him, but not often. He claimed to try to read to both his parents sometimes. At school he was now beginning to read the Gay Way Red Book and when he was older he would read the Blue Book. He knew about other people reading and about the framework within which he expected to learn, but his own learning was rather a mystery. By the end of his third year he was not convinced that reading mattered in the early school years because other children were managing without being able to read. Nevertheless, he thought it would matter later in schoolwork. He was also aware throughout that both his parents and his teachers wanted and expected him to read, though he did not seem to find their concern a burden.

He understood something of the act of authorship in writing, even on starting school. He was able to copy and write freely, both neatly and accurately, and drew on his own ideas from outside the core words in the Breakthrough scheme, but he was not able to write directly. He needed to be provided with the words he suggested, and, even when he had them available in front of him and could recognise each, he was not able to write a new combination of his own making without first building the sentence with word cards and then copying it. He also forgot words rather readily, and it seemed his reading and writing were affected by difficulty in holding in mind the relationship between a word and its visual image. By his second year, however, he was able to write directly from his own ideas provided he had previously seen the words involved. He could suggest and write sentences like *Witches fly around at night* and *I have got a kite. It is red.* By the end of the year he was willing to venture into writing words he was not familiar with, thus producing such interesting spellings as *Nuws* for *Noah's.* All in all there seemed to be no lack of understanding of reading and writing behind Sean's relatively slow reading progress, though his perception of the size of the task and his lack of intrinsic motivation to learn might have had a combined delaying effect.

Equally there was no evidence of any language problem. His score on the English Picture Vocabulary test was well above the norm, and was third highest in his class. When talking he could depict events and combine them in a clear sequential account, while his story-telling had narrative structure and entertainment emphasis. Although his local dialect was strong he modified it towards 'text' in story-retelling. His explanations and use of terms expressing possibility and uncertainty were entirely adequate and were combined with a good conceptual understanding for his age. He was not shy and talked readily with his teachers.

His difficulties with reading were not unrelated to the development of his grasp of English orthography, and it is worth tracing the two together. In Tests A2 and A3 (Appendix A) he showed knowledge of numbers and letters (named phonically) but less idea of the terms *letter, word* and *sentence* than that shown by some of the other children. This suggested less attention to the terminology of reading instruction than expected, considering his experience at home and in school, and, by implication, less attention to 'text' of any kind. This would give a very poor basis for beginning to build some implicit knowledge of the spelling system.

Lack of attention to words would also account for his poor recognition of them during his first year. He sought words in his Breakthrough work, but then failed to remember them. Initially he constructed a much more varied and personal sentence-book than most of the other children but, in spite of the interest in generating them, he seemed to be content to store them in his book rather than in his head, and on later occasions could not re-read them.

His ability to see and discriminate pattern in words was nevertheless strong. During the interview A4 (Appendix A) he read the word *Meg* among others and, when asked how he knew it was Meg, he replied that it had *M* and all the letters in to say *Meg.* He seemed to mean that it contained three letters and that he knew *Meg* had three letters. He may also have meant it had the right three letters. He also judged *cat* and *dog* to be unlike, but *house* and *home* to have *h, o* and *e* the same. He liked making sentences with his Breakthrough folder and suggested *I went home for my dinner*. He managed *I went home* (a recent construction) but needed help with the last part of the sentence. There were no order problems. He read *I am a boy* and judged it to be a sentence, and also read correctly *am I a boy* and *boy am a I*, judging neither to be a sentence. For the former he said that nobody did it like that, and for the latter he said the *I* should be at the other end. He was therefore well aware of the significance of word order and of left–right ordering for reading; and, like Wilma, John and Mary, had a strong expectation – almost a rule – that *I* came at the beginning of sentences.

The Breakthrough reading test at the end of the second term found Sean still in the predicament of being unable to remember many words. He was successful only with *a*, *big*, *I*, *little*, *is* and *see*. His errors showed appreciation of graphic similarities of word length and some two-letter patterns, as in *cat* for *can* (and vice versa), *in* for *at* and *red* for *are*. He attempted some sounding, without success; and his sentence reading was no better than word reading, except for a self-correction of *cat* to the appropriate word *can*. The juxtaposition of *can* with *I* in a sentence seemed to be a useful cue. *Television* was misread as *little*, again an error with graphic similarity. If once told the missing words, however, he had no trouble re-reading the sentences correctly. But in June he read sixteen words in the same test. This was a considerable improvement, suggesting that his recognition skills had somehow received a boost. He tried sounding with some success, and his misreadings included similarly spelled words. Visual memory seemed to be improving with the attention to detail required in a phonic approach, but the connection was not necessarily causal.

In reading variously composed lists and sentences from the First Red Book in June, Sean proved to be the least able of the four of the ten children who were in a position to attempt the task. He either read correctly or omitted words, making only one misreading – *hill* for *fell* – in a word list. Sentences formed from parts of sentences in the book were no better read than word lists; but exact copies and internally rearranged versions of sentences from the book were better read. The exact copies were read better than the novel, the advantage seeming to lie with words like *up*, *the*, *and* and *a* which were probably read as part of the better-learned whole, that is, as a remembered sentence, rather than as individual words.

In July his reading aloud from the Second Red Book was observed and recorded. The edited transcript follows (age 5 years 4 months).

Ben the dog ran to the top of the hill. He ran up to the old red lorry. Ben jumped up (at) to the t-o-p, top of the old lorry. Bang. He fell down into the lorry. Jip the cat ran to the (lorry) top of* the hill. She ran up to the old red lorry. She jumped up (on to the lorry) (to) on the lorry and sat down. (In) Who* is in the lorry? I am in the l-o . . . lorry. I am Ben the dog. I fell in. Bang. Jip the cat jumped up and fell down into the lorry.

At first sight Sean seems to have been reading quite well. There are few mistakes. Except for the supply of *of* at his request and *Who* when he misread it as *In*, mistakes were self-corrected. But in fact he did not find reading easy. Only the first three sentences were read at all smoothly – having been read before. The rest was read jerkily and often word by word. There was little attempt at phonic analysis, but rather a consistent effort to remember the words. Self-correction was seen to be needed when the sense was carried on but then led to nonsense. The error was seen and the correct word used, and one gained the impression that the word-by-word approach allowed this to happen. A rather interesting incident occurred with the penultimate reading of *lorry*. The sense did not help Sean, who in fact tried a phonic attack and began *l o*, but at that point recognised the word and said, not *lorry* as one might have expected, but *rolly*, which was his way of articulating *lorry* throughout. Presumably a full phonic analysis would have yielded *lorry*, but it would not have been Sean's most natural way of saying it. Yet this minor articulation eccentricity did not affect his reading.

Over the year Sean had not made the advances in reading that his initial progress had suggested. He seemed to show many of the subskills of value; but he had great difficulty in retaining the visual impression of words, and his progress was rather like filling a bucket with a hole in the bottom. While more might be added, the earlier volume ran away. Yet progress was being made, and unless Sean became daunted, he might suffer nothing worse than a relative delay in these early stages. Whether more intensive consolidation of learning of words might have been a means of blocking the holes one cannot really say. The difficulty might not have been so readily resolved.

Early in his second year he tackled Test B2 (Appendix B) with interest and care. He easily identified big and little words and recognised similar letters, naming them phonically. He readily identified similar two-letter patterns at the beginning of words and went on to 'sound' the words. Two- and three-letter patterns at the ends of words taxed his skill, however, and here his attention wandered. He settled for single-letter matching, but central double letters *oo* and *ee* were easily matched. He enjoyed the sentence completion item and responded well. But in a further attempt at the Breakthrough test he did no better than six months previously. He read fourteen words correctly, omitted *boy, girl, good, big, baby, he, birthday, we, school, my* and *are*. He misread *television* as *little, dog* as *big* and then *got, like* as *little, home* as *make* and *can* as *cat*, but then he did correct this last himself. The misreadings suggested graphic similarity errors, and this, with the lack of improvement in score and the variability of his success with particular words, suggested some inadequately cued access to memory. This had been other children's state a year earlier.

A sample of Sean's reading in early November from the Third Red Book is given below.

Extract from the Third Red Book (Gay Way)
Get the back off the lorry, Bang, bang, bang, bang went Sam and the fat pig. Bang, bang, bang, bang went Jip and Ben. Ting, ting, ting, ting went Deb and Meg. Get the wheels off the lorry. Bang, bang, bang, bang went Sam and the fat pig. Bang, bang, bang, bang, went Jip and Ben. Ting, ting, ting, ting went Deb and Meg. Who will make the new house? I will make the walls, said the fat pig. Bang, bang, bang, bang. The fat pig made the walls of the new house.

Sean's reading (age 5 years 8 months)
Get the b-a-c-k, b-a-c-k, back off the lorry.
(Sean then read the next three sentences without halt or error.)
Get the w-h-e-e-l-s, wheels* off the lorry.
(Next three sentences with no halt or error.)
W-h-o, Who* will ma . . . mak-e, make the new house? I will (said) m . . . make the (house) (w-e-l, well) (windows) walls*, said the fat pig. Bang, bang, bang, bang. The fat pig ma-b . . . ma-d . . . made the walls of the new house.

Sean was having some success with sounding, but needed help where there was not a one-to-one grapheme–phoneme correspondence, as in the cases of *ee* and *wh*. In trying to read *walls* he first confused it with his memory of *wheels*, the graphic similarity even leading him to see *a* as *e*, and then with *windows*, which also combined a *w . . . s* pattern with possible sense. He had to tackle it with greater attention to the particular word, for which he needed help.

A further sample of his reading in November from the Third Red Book is given below.

Extract from the Third Red Book (Gay Way)
Who will get the chimney pot for the new house? It is down the hill. I will get it, said Meg the hen. So Meg went to get the chimney pot.

Sean's reading (Age 5 years 8 months)
Who will get the chimney pot (of) f-o-r, for* the new house? It is down (to) on the hill. I will (said) get it, said Meg the hen. So Meg went to get the chimney pot.

Sean still read slowly and rather jerkily, but fluently enough for the listener to 'feel' the meaning. He was able to correct by himself those errors which were sense-guessing or anticipatory errors, and only needed help with *for* when sounding did not cue him sufficiently. He now read *Who* without hesitation.

A similar sampling in December revealed little else of interest, except that he continued to be guided by context in both producing and correcting misreadings, the corrections obviously indicating attention to some visual cue from the text. He had some success with sounding new and forgotten words, managing *ring* entirely by himself.

Some slow progress was evident by February.

Extract from the Fourth Red Book (Gay Way)
Deb the rat and Meg the hen went down the hill. Deb and Meg went to see old man Tod. He lived in the old house with the red chimney pot and the brown door.

Sean's reading (Age 5 years 11 months)
Deb the rat and Meg the hen (and) went down the hill. Deb and Meg went to see old man Tod. He lived in the old house w-i-t-h, w-i-th*, with the red (dog) (windows) (wheels) c-h . . . ch-i-m* . . . chimney-pot and the (down) dr-o . . . br-ow . . . brown door.

He stumbled at four points, the first being an error of expectancy, based on a familiar sequence, which he very quickly corrected by himself. The second led him to ask for help. He was encouraged to sound it, and it became clear that he needed help with the *th* ending. This was given and Sean easily blended the sounds to read *with*. At the third he guessed wildly (all three guesses being possible in terms of syntax and sense) but then settled to try to read the word correctly. He needed help with the *ch* beginning and then read the rest of the word without difficulty. At the fourth he misread *brown* as *down*, obviously reading *b* as *d*, but also taking up the similarity in the two words. Once he had the *b* correct he read the word easily. His intonation was good, his sound-blending quick, and his taking-up of cues from a variety of sources was helpful. He responded quickly to help with sounding. But his reading was rather slow, and he still pointed to each word as he read. The nature of his misreadings suggested that he may have needed to be slow and steady at this stage, in order to identify words accurately.

Another reading was recorded in May.

Extract from the Fifth Red Book (Gay Way)

So they went on till they came to the new house. Ben the dog and Jip the cat sat by the door. Hello, hello, children. Hello, old woman. Hello, Jip. Hello, Ben. Can we live in the new house? No, old woman. We live in the new house with Meg the hen, Deb the rat, Sam the fox and the fat pig. You have so many children. You cannot live in the new house.

Sean's reading (age 6 years 2 months)

So (the-n) (then) they went on till they came to the new house. Ben the dog and Jip the cat sat (be) (my) (been) by the door. Hello, hello, children. Hello, old woman. Hello, Jip. Hello, Ben. (Come) c-a-n, can we live in the new house? No, old woman. We live in the new house (then) with Meg the hen, Deb the rat, Sam the fox and the fat pig. (Yes) y-o-u, y-ou* you have so many children. You (can live . . . No!) cannot live in (this) the new house.

This was read confidently, with considerable expression, but a little jerkily. Errors seemed to be due to visual similarity as with *they*, *then* and *with*, *be*, *my* and *by*, *come* and *can*, and *yes* and *you*. All were self-corrected, however, with context and sounding cues to help. Only at one point was help needed – with *ou* in *you*. Although Sean was obviously making progress with his reading, his skill did not match John's and Wilma's, and was marginally poorer than Mary's. His standardised test scores, giving him a reading age below the norm, seemed a fair assessment.

By the end of his first term in his third year, however, he was doing rather better.

Reading from the Sixth Red Book (Age 6 years 8 months)

The big dog, the little cat and Tod (get in the lorry) got in. The lorry man got in. He shu . . . shut the door. (Big) Bang. Go back

to the water. Go back up the hill. Go down the hill. Go to old man
Tod's house, said the old woman.
So the lorry man went back to the water and up the hill. Then he
went down the hill and on to Tod's house.
Stop the lorry, said the old woman. Get out, children.

Here there was little error, and Sean needed no help. He recognised
his own mistake in running the first sentence into the second, and
sorted it out. He started to sound *shut* so smoothly that he immediately grasped the word, and he corrected his misreading of
Bang. From that point on he read the next items rather jerkily,
which is not perhaps surprising, and then settled into a fluent
reading of the longer sentences. He was asked to read the next page
by himself – which he did, quietly, but still aloud. Afterwards he was
able to give a sensible version of what he had read.

Some insight into his reading was gained through Tests C1 and C2
(Appendix C). In the former he failed to classify any of the words as
'made-up English'. Either they were English or they were foreign,
and only half of the true English words were recognised as such.
Sean was making a conceptual distinction not based on the visual
evidence before him, except in so far as the written words conveyed
meanings to him. In spite of his visual-perceptual skills there was no
suggestion of recognition of permitted and non-permitted orthographic patterns. Further, even the phonic skills which Sean sometimes brought to bear on his reading were not used to rule out the
non-English items. His performance on the word card sorting test
(C2, Appendix C) was rather different, however, for he did try
some sounding and was thus persuaded to include three nonsense
syllables in his choice of English words. This in no way altered the
conclusion that he was not demonstrating the sort of awareness of
English orthography that had been shown by John, and to some
extent by Wilma and Mary. Insufficient attention to the graphic
structure of words when attempting to read, or some difficulty in
storing and retrieving information, might have been involved,
though memory difficulties would themselves affect attention. Certainly visual memory had seemed to be a possible problem in Sean's
first year. So had some attentional difficulty which now seemed
evident in his *e*-cancelling in Test C3, for although he approached
the task much more carefully than John, he missed almost as many
*e*s. Although he missed proportionately more non-sounded *e*s than
sounded, whether this was due in his case to a more phonic
approach or whether, as with the other children, it showed a
sensitivity to different orthographic patterning, was not clear. It
seemed possible that the other children were able to use orthog-

raphic knowledge as a means of coming to an explicit phonic analysis, while Sean was using sounding as a way of familiarising himself with orthography.

By February his reading had taken him into the Green Book series, but he was still having to correct himself over quite simple words, as is shown in the transcript below (age 6 years 11 months).

> So the girl said to the fat pig, Come and help us to pull up the very big turnip.
> The fat pig (come) came and (help) h-e-l-d, held on to the girl and the boy and the old woman and the old man. (Then) They pulled and pulled. But they could not pull up the very big turnip.

One error in the above reading, and not one easily shown, was the substitution of *could not* for *couldn't*. The latter was the text version, while the former matched Sean's typical use in his speech. In general the reading was accurate but obviously still more like that of Wilma and John at an earlier age. Sean reported that he did not now like reading much, and did not read other books available in the classroom for private reading. Sometimes he could not read words in his number and other work.

It seemed possible that the Daniels and Diack diagnostic tests might throw some light on Sean's difficulty. His score on the basic test gave a reading age of 6½ years, which meant that he was about nine months behind the norm. As in previous copying and drawing tasks, his performance in copying abstract designs and a sentence was good. His work was neater and more accurate than that of any other child in the sample. His performance on the test of visual discrimination and orientation was excellent, though he also sounded words in the word matching part of the test. All his responses to the letter recognition and the aural discrimination tests were correct. It was only in the various parts of the diagnostic word recognition tests that he began to make mistakes. Even in the simple word test he gave two misreadings, apparently confusing single letters in final positions, such as *t* for *x* and *d* for *b*. This kind of error occurred again, but in a relatively mild form, in later tests. His blending of consonants in initial and final positions was faultless, and he managed to read the polysyllabic, phonically simple words satisfactorily, albeit slowly. He had more trouble with phonically more complex and irregularly spelled words, which was not surprising; and, more interestingly, he made errors with 'reversible' words, giving *tud* for *tub* and *dad* for *dab*, and with nonsense syllables, giving *sad* for *sab*, *stid* for *stib* and *veld* for *velb*. These are all single-letter misreadings where the letter *d* was read for *b* in final positions. There were no other letter or word reversals and *b* was read correctly in other positions. In the oral word recognition test he made only two mistakes, both showing a 'next-best' graphic similarity to the desired word, and he made three similar mistakes in the picture word recognition test. In neither case was a letter misreading apparent. How did Sean's difficulty with reading relate to a single-letter problem? And why was *b* confused with *d*, and in the final position only, when he gave no other sign of orientation difficulty? True, he had occasionally confused *b* and *d* in his writing during his three years in the school, but he had shown few signs of misreading *b* in his everyday reading. Perhaps the errors held little diagnostic value apart from highlighting the attention to detail needed to discriminate between similar words.

By the end of this year he had progressed to the Blue Book from which the following was read (age 7 years 3 months).

One day the red fox met the (greedy) grey wolf.
Red Fox said (greedy) Grey Wolf, Will you let me come and live with you? I will chop the sticks for the fire. I will wash up. I will make the beds and sweep the floor. (I . . . What . . .) And what do you want me to do, said Red Fox. You will go out and get the dinner, said the (greedy) grey wolf. The fox (said) did not know that the wolf was very greedy. He (looked to eat) liked to eat all day long.

Sean read steadily, with intonation, but also with some jerkiness, repetition and a false start. He found it hard to prevent himself reading *greedy wolf* instead of *grey wolf*, but corrected himself each time. His other errors, *said* for *did* and *looked* for *liked*, were graphically similar misreadings. His grasp of the story was good, in that when asked to recall it he did so fairly accurately and giving the gist of it.

The reader may have noticed that this sample was also read by Wilma six months earlier with some very similar errors. Sean was obviously in a position to make headway now, in spite of his slow progress at first. His teacher reported that his number work was very good and that his reading and writing were adequate for general instructional purposes, though his free writing tended to be brief. He made overt use of phonics in both reading and writing. What had yet to develop was a fluency beyond an overt dependence on word recognition and phonics. Perhaps what Sean had missed throughout his learning to read was sufficient practice with, and attention to, text. Although he was intelligent and interested, he had neither John's interest in text meanings, nor Wilma's persistence, to provide the necessary personal motivation to scan for pattern and to attend to detail in order to discriminate between patterns. Either he suffered some processing deficit in access to visual memory, or he had not given himself sufficient chance to develop much knowledge of the English spelling system.

DAVE

Dave was a rather quiet, somewhat reserved 5-year-old, with fine small features and a slender build. He attended school regularly and showed no particular physical or health problems, but he began drawing and writing at school with his left hand and later changed to his right. He was the only child of parents who both worked for British Rail – his father as a shunter and his mother as a carriage cleaner. At first he was quietly friendly with other children and rarely in trouble. He seemed to float with the stream rather than actively make his own way in the classroom in his first year, but in his second and third years he became more actively involved in a friendship group where he was seen as a 'real lad' who could occasionally be aggressive. He did not find it easy to learn to read, but his comments about his experiences at home suggested that this was not because he was without support. He spoke of his parents reading, of his mother reading aloud to him sometimes, and of his efforts to read to her. His comments were consistent during the two years of the study, but because it was not possible to interview his mother their accuracy could not be confirmed. Nor was it possible to gain any information about his approach to reading before coming to school.

His understanding of reading and writing as revealed in Test A4 (Appendix A) seemed limited but not absent. He was quite sure that he could not yet read, but thought that when he was bigger he would read like some older person he mentioned, but whose relationship to himself he could not make clear. Yet he had no idea of what he might then read. He reported that his father read the paper and books, but that his mother did not. He had a 'Goosey Gander' book at home and his mother read aloud to him sometimes, but not very often, and he sometimes tried to read to her. What he meant by this was not clear. When shown a copy of the Gay Way Red Book he could read nothing in it, but he did observe that pictures did not help much because 'it was all in the writing'. This was quite a significant insight into the dual arts of reading and writing but, as will be seen later, he had no idea of text as a stable source of information.

His own writing skill developed so slowly that there was little evidence of the nature of his understanding of authorship. The most that can be said is that he stayed within the field of the Breakthrough scheme and brought little of his own ideas from outside it. It was possible that he defined learning to read and write as school activities, not much, if at all, related to reading and writing in the outside world.

By the end of his second year, when interviewed about reading, Dave was less certain than the other children about liking it. His answer was: 'Yes, but not a lot.' He liked it because 'You learn' – an answer that seemed to indicate a restricted idea of coming to grips with a task. He referred to books at home, including one about Pinocchio, and to the Third Red Book at school. He said, with honesty and insight, that he found it hard to remember words. After two years he claimed to be sounding when trying to read a word he had forgotten, but not when trying new words. For these he did nothing, and this strongly suggested a reproductive rather than a discovery attitude to reading. He did not think reading was useful to older children or adults, though he did think it was useful to his age-group to help them to read better. Reading was an end, but not a means to any other end. He felt his parents and teachers all wanted him to learn, and he reported that his mother now helped him by listening to him. Moreover, in spite of his hesitancy about liking reading, he said he would like to read more in school, by himself, if he could. Dave's rather confused views of reading and writing may have affected his approach to them and his rate of learning, but they were not so inadequate as to leave him totally uncertain about what he was at.

Similarly he did not seem to suffer any disabling language deficit, though his speech tended to consist of rather concise remarks and he was not inclined to talk much with his teachers, or to seek help from them. Perhaps the more limiting aspects of his abilities showed in his story-telling and in the English Picture Vocabulary test. His stories showed sequential structure but little thematic coherence, and his vocabulary score was about the norm. That conceptual rather than linguistic abilities might be somewhat limited was also indicated in his responses to Test B5 (Appendix B). He was able to use the various terms appropriately as far as linguistic structures were concerned, and expressed himself clearly, but showed lack of understanding compared with some of the other children. But in no sense could he be said to be performing below the average for his age, so it seemed unlikely that slowness in learning to read could be attributed to language deficiencies.

Dave's development of knowledge of English spelling came very slowly. He was able to discriminate letters from numbers in Test A2 (Appendix A), but unable to name any; while in Test A3 he showed much confusion over the terms *sentence*, *word* and *letter*. This indicated little experience of relating such terms to text in the course of learning, either in class or at home, and made it seem unlikely that he had attended sufficiently to written words of any kind for any implicit appreciation of visual pattern. Moreover his copying of words and even of 'pre-writing patterns' was erratic in a way that suggested that it was unlikely that he expected pattern or regularity.

Nevertheless, he began to grow familiar with aspects of the Breakthrough work. By the end of his second term in school he was able to read the sentence in his folder *I am at school* and to judge it to be a sentence; and he read correctly the rearranged versions *am I at school* and *school am I at*. He judged neither to be sentences, saying that the former was the wrong way round while the latter should start with *I*. Obviously a sentence meant more to him that a string of words. He also had some visual analytic skill in that he judged *dog* and *cat* to be not the same, while *home* and *house* were alike because each had *h*, *o* and *e*. He could not read the words or name the letters, but indicated his judgements by pointing. In the Breakthrough word test (Test A5, Appendix A) at the end of the second term he read *television*, *cat*, *I* and *am*, and made no other attempts. When reading the sentences, however, he also read *see* and *dog*, and misread *my* as *am* – a graphic similarity. But he also mistakenly read *television* as *school*, *dog* as *mum*, and almost entirely misread the last sentence as *I am a ball*. Only *I* was correct. It seemed that he sometimes guessed to such an extent that he failed to see words (for example, *television*) that he could read correctly. His guesswork seemed to be influenced by the sort of sentences he had encountered in classwork – not freely drawn from speech. There was some attempt to sound words but this was entirely unsuccessful, for he could make no transitions from a sounded pattern to an actual word. With the same test a month or two later he managed to read *can*, *cat*, *at*, *I* and *see* successfully, especially drawing on sounding for *can*, *cat* and *at*. He was therefore showing signs not only of knowing about a phonic approach but also of being able to use one. He had, however, forgotten words; and he guessed *television* for *house*, *dad* for *television*, *am* for *a* and *cat* for *are*. Perhaps there was some graphic similarity in some cases, but in others there seemed to be no accounting for his misreading.

In July, when he was 5 years 4 months old, an attempt to read was observed and recorded. Dave had not begun to work with the Gay Way books, and he volunteered to read from a classroom copy of the Ladybird book *Peter and Jane*, a copy of which he said he read at home. The following transcript gives both Dave's and the observer's remarks, and brackets the actual text and additional comments for the reader's information.

D: That's Peter. (*Peter* – single word with picture)
O: That's good.
D: That's Jane. (*Jane* – new page with picture)
D: That's Peter and Jane. (*Peter and Jane* – new page with picture)
O: Yes, can you point to the word that says *and*? Can you put your finger on it?
D: And? (Dave is surprised. He has been reading from the pictures, not the words.)
O: The word that says *and*. (No response)
O: Can you put your finger on the word that says *Peter*?
D: Peter. (Places finger on correct word)
O: Good. Can you put your finger on the word that says *Jane*? (Dave does so)
O: Good. Now which is the one that says *and*?
D: And. (Pointing to it)
O: Good. You were looking at the picture first, weren't you?
D: Yes.
O: Let's try some more. Can you read any of that? (Turning to a new page, again with a picture)
D: Peter and Jane. (Points correctly to *Peter*)
   (The actual sentence was *Here is Peter and Here is Jane.*)
O: Which is *Jane*? (Dave points correctly)
   Good. Can you find an *and* there?
D: And?
O: Yes, you remember there was one on the other page, wasn't there? Let's have a look. (Turns back)
D: I'll tell you which it isn't. It's them two. (Pointing to *Peter* and *Jane*)
O: Yes, so that was *and*, wasn't it? (Pointing) Now can you find it on the next page? (Turns forward again)
D: It's there. (Pointing correctly)
O: Yes, of course it is. It's exactly like the other one.
   Now, do you know what that is? (Pointing to *Here*)
D: That? No.
O: That's *here*. Can you find another *here* on that page?
D: An 'ere?
D: Here. (Pointing correctly)
O: Yes, good. So we've got *Here is Peter and* . . .
D: Here's Jane. (Note ellipsis)
O: Yes. Here is Jane. (Turns over page to new picture)

D: It's the seaside here. (Reads) Here is Peter building – I mean digging a sandcastle. (This is read word by word, pointing – but the actual text is *Peter is here and Jane is here!*)

Dave actually went on reading for another three pages with help, and could only remember *Peter*, *Jane* and *dog*. His attempts to read were therefore based on these words and the pictures. He kept forgetting all other words in spite of being able to see likeness and identities, and he did not attempt sounding. One wondered whether he expected most words to change meaning with context. In his comments he said he found it hard to remember words, but the pictures helped. This was a shift from his earlier view about pictures, and may have meant some recognition of his own position as a learner. He also said this time that if he wanted help he would ask the teacher.

This very passive attempt to read was quite like his general work in class. He did not show any particular competence and, while willing to try what was asked of him, seemed often to do so without much understanding of what school activities were about. Certainly he did not seem to have grasped that a particular arrangement of words in text normally carried a stable meaning for the reader.

By the beginning of his second year in school Dave's copying skills had improved and his free writing, such as it was, was better formed. He had difficulty with more complex pattern copying and this, like his reading, may have been related to some difficulty in coping with much visual information from abstract figures at any one time. His performance in Test B2 (Appendix B) was quite good, but he identified double- and triple-letter patterns by taking one letter at a time. He still had only a few words in his Breakthrough folder, and so little in the way of either an internal or an external pool of information about English spelling.

Later that term, however, he had begun to add the early sentences from the Gay Way Red Book to his repertoire. A transcript of one of his attempts to start reading the book is given below.

Extract from the First Red Book (Gay Way)
The big red lorry went up the hill. The pots and pans went up the hill in the lorry. Big pans, little pans.

Dave's reading (Age 5 years 8 months)
The big red lorry went up the hill. The (pa) (big) pots* and* (big) pans* went* up the hill in the* lorry. Big (and) (pot) pans*, little pans.

Dave seemed to be reading one word at a time on an all-or-none word recognition basis. His misreadings had elements of visual similarity with the correct words. He made no attempts to sound words he could not recognise, nor did he seem able to try when it was suggested, which was strange considering his attempts a few months ago. Consequently he was told all the asterisked words.

In December a further recording of his reading from the First Red Book was taken. He was then almost 6.

Extract from the First Red Book (Gay Way)
Big pans, little pans, big pots and little pots. Red pans, tin pans, red pots and tin pots. Up and up to the top went the big red lorry. Up and up and up went the pots. Up went the pans.

Dave's reading (Age 5 years 9 months)
Big (pots) (p-o) No! P-a . . . pans. Big pans, little pans, big pots and* little pots. Red (pots) p-a . . . pans, t-i-n, tin (pots) pans, red (pans) p-o . . . pots and t-i-n, tin pots. Up and up (the) to the t-o-p, (pots) t-o-p, top (of) w-e-n-t, went (up) the big red lorry. Up and up and up went (up) the (lorry) p-o-t-s, pots. Up went the pans.

When Dave's attention was drawn to his first error with *pans* he tried to sound the word, at first incorrectly, but then successfully. This was all his own effort. Subsequently he sorted *pots* and *pans* and *tin* and *top* by sounding without its being suggested to him. He was delighted with his success. His reading errors suggested an approach influenced by expectations from other reading, or simply from sense. He was helped with the *w* in *went* and his omission of *and*, but his misreadings entailing running on with *the*, *of*, *up* and *lorry* were self-corrected. He was therefore seen to be attending to the text and the sense as well as being influenced by memories of other sentences. Other children had been doing this a year earlier.

Further progress was made during the next couple of months and in February another recording was made.

Reading from the First Red Book (Gay Way) (Age 5 years 11 months)
I am Deb the little rat. Can I live in the (tin) pot, Ben? You can live in (the) it* Deb. (Sat) So* Meg the hen, and Jip the cat, and Sam the fox, and Ben the dog, and Deb the little rat lived* in the tin pot house (the) on* the hill.

Dave's reading scarcely needed a transcription, for he made only five errors. His reading carried intonation and was fairly smooth, but it was very slow and each word was stressed. There was a suggestion of some graphic similarity in three errors. In the second sentence *tin* was read for *pot*, an error which also suggested an incorrect anticipation. This was self-corrected. In the third sentence *the* was read for *it*, but help was needed to read *it*. When, in the next sentence, *Sat* was read for *So*, the common *S* may have had an effect. Dave read *So* with help in sounding the long vowel. He also needed help with *lived*, where he was not clear about the sounds for *l* and *v* and confused them with *r*. His last error, reading *the* for *on* seemed unaccountable, but when he tried sounding he produced *o-t* and the *t/n* difference had to be pointed out. To some extent, then, Dave's knowledge of the sounds of letters seemed insecure, but his word recognition was not bad and he was able to blend sounds to make words he recognised.

A further sample of reading was made in May.

Extract from the Second Red Book (Gay Way)
I am Deb the little rat. I went ting, ting, ting, I will get in. Can I live in the shoe? I have no house to live in.

Dave's reading (Age 6 years 2 months)
I am Deb the little rat. I (will) w-e-n-t. went ting, ting, ting. I will get in. Can I (like) live in the (old) sh-o-e, shoe*. I h-a-v-e, have* no house to live in.

This was another very slow, word-by word reading, but errors were few. There was graphic similarity in *will* for *went*, *like* for *live*, and both errors fitted sensibly with what had gone before. It was presumably the sight of the word to come that cued Dave to try again. He tried sounding *went*, but recognised *live* at the second try. There may have been a recognition of the common *o* in *shoe* and *old*, but this error seemed probably an anticipation mistake based on earlier sentences in the book. He needed help with *have*, his sounding of the final *e* blocking his realisation of the word. In spite of his slow approach he showed a grasp of visual, phonic and sense cues. He even knew the sound for *sh*. Essentially his difficulty seemed to lie with getting sufficient perceptual grasp of some kind to recognise each word.

By the time he started his third year in school Dave was still finding reading very difficult. When seen in November he was working at a very elementary level at the first of the Sound Sense series, finding words with *i* to name items in a picture which contained so many examples it was difficult to find one without an *i*. His writing of the words he chose was large and erratic. His reading at that time was from the Third Red Book in the Gay Way series, and he used a card to define each line as he read. The following extract was recorded, the asterisks showing where he was helped (age 6 years 8 months).

> Sam the fox and the (big) fat pig c-a-m, (come) came* d-o-w, down the hill to the tree (went) w-i-t-h, with* the old red lorry. Ben the dog and Jip the cat came up the hill to the tree. Deb the rat and Meg the hen came up the hill to the tree with the old shoe house.

Dave read slowly, mostly word by word, but with some phrasing. He was able to correct his misreading of *fat* without help, but he was not able to find his own way to *came* and *with*, where the silent *e* rule and digraph *th* defeated him. Nevertheless, he was willing to try sounding and was successful with *down*. When he was asked to read without his line indicator, he did so, pointing to each word as he read, and with no apparent loss in performance.

As a matter of interest he was asked to try Test C1 (Appendix C), which he quite enjoyed in his own way. He seemed not to understand the idea of a non-English or foreign word, but to accept that 'made-up English' had some meaning, so that he sorted words into the 'real' and the 'made-up'. The result was that half his 'real' category were familiar English words, and the remainder were nonsense syllables and non-permitted letter combinations. A post-test exploration showed that he misread all these as familiar English words. He was apparently not sufficiently aware of the regularities of orthography to reject the non-English, and was still tending to make the graphic similarity errors characteristic of very early attempts to read. His choices in Test C2 (Appendix C) showed no discrimination between English and non-English and therefore confirmed his lack of orthographic knowledge. In neither task did he attempt to read words by sounding them.

He performed the *e*-cancelling task with the same level of care as Sean and Mary, but his omissions tended to be of mid-position letters and of some final. He seemed to notice letters that were salient by virtue of their first position, doubling of the vowel, or final position in short words. This again was characteristic of very early reading, and showed neither orthographic knowledge nor phonic skill.

By February, when he was 7, he had progressed to the First Green Book in the Gay Way series, but he reported little interest in reading either at home or school. Although his mother sometimes read his book to him he did not try to read to her, and in school he preferred to draw or copy. The following extract from his book was read slowly, word by word, and with a finger pointing to each (age 6 years 11 months).

> Jo is a cat. He (has) had no house to live in, so he lived in the s-t-r-e-e-t, street. He had to (stay, stop) s-i-t, sit in the street. He had to sleep in the street. Jo, y-o-u, you are the old street-cat.

This time Dave corrected all his misreadings and managed to use sounding to some effect, even for *ee* and *ou*. But there were few words that he had not seen and tried to read for the best part of two years. It seemed rather strange that sounding was being used for what should have been familiar words. This was true to some extent for Sean and Mary, but was very marked in Dave's case.

The Daniels and Diack basic reading test showed how little progress he had made, for his score was more than a year below the norm. Unlike the better readers, his copying of abstract figures in the diagnostic tests was very inaccurate, though his work was neat enough. This suggested a need for more progress with perceptual discrimination skill as a means of strengthening his reading. His sentence copying was more accurate but with no separation of words, this again pointing to a weakness in perceptual skill.

His performance in the visual matching task was good, however, showing no orientation problems in his perception, and his letter recognition in word-initial and final positions was also accurate, while his performance on the aural discrimination test was also error-free.

The various word recognition tests were tedious for him, however, and he was so slow in reading the items that he was not taken through all of them. He made graphic similarity errors in the simple phonically regular words and found consonant blending at the beginning of words difficult, though he managed blending at the end of words more easily. He also found polysyllabic words hard, in spite of correct sounding, and seemed to have no knowledge of digraphs such as *ch*, *th*, *sh*, nor of patterns such as *er* and *ate*. He misread many of the irregularly spelled familiar words, and the words and nonsense syllables intended to be used to check for reversals. All were misreadings of a non-reversal kind. In the oral and picture word recognition tests he did rather better, with only one or two errors. His main weakness seemed, therefore, to lie in accurately perceiving the integration of detail in complex patterns, and in an associated lack of experience in reading. The former had

been evident from the earliest observations, but, while some training had been given to all the children, there had been no special
treatment for particular weakness.

In the final term of his third year his teacher reported that his
phonic skill was quite good and that he was willing to try free writing
(although it was phonically spelled and rather messy). His oral
number work was also good, but his reading was still only progressing slowly. He had moved on to the First Blue Book, from
which the following sample was read (age 7 years 3 months).

> Then the robin went to the red hen who sat on her nest in the tin
> house.
> Did you take my eggs away? I lost six out of my nest today.
> Cut cut, cut cut, cut cut, cut, went the little red hen.
> No, I did not. Ben the dog gave you a bit of his coat for your nest. I
> gave you my soft feathers.* But I did not take your six eggs out of
> (the) your nest. Cut cut, cut cut, cut cut, cut. I did not. I did not.

There were only two errors, *the* being corrected by Dave himself,
and *fur* being read instead of *feathers*, an error he was not able to
correct without help. Yet he had read words which implied some
mastery of more complex skill than he had shown in earlier reading
or in the Daniels and Diack test. Possibly he was not able to
generalise his skill yet beyond very familiar words, and the text
would in any case help him to hazard a word he was uncertain about,
but he was indubitably reading a little better than before. Although
he still tended to read word by word rather than with phrased
intonation, he was able to show afterwards that he had understood
what he had read. It seemed possible, if his basic intelligence could
be linked with an interest in extending his reading and developing
his writing, that he might make up some of the difference that now
existed between his skill and that of his more successful peers. But,
being nearly two years behind the norm, he was obviously vulnerable to feelings of frustration and dejection. He was nearly 8, but
needed the intensive support usually given to 6-year-olds.

SUMMARY

After reviewing these three cases it might be useful to ask what the
children shared with the more successful readers and how they
differed from them.

In common with John and Wilma, they did not lack support for
reading at home, though it was not pressed upon them. There was
little evidence of considering learning to read before going to

school, and the range of available reading materials seemed small. In addition there was a strong flavour of their seeing reading as something to do with starting school rather than an ability to be valued throughout life, and as something that could or could not be done rather than a constantly developing skill. Motivation to learn was therefore less strong than in John, who was always 'pressing to know', and in Wilma, who liked to do things thoroughly. At times motivation was not only low but rather negative, Mary, for example, not being inclined to take up the support she might have had at home, and Sean positively preferring to spend his time in other ways.

Like John and Wilma, the three children started to learn to recognise a limited set of words which were combined in simple sentences in their Breakthrough experience. They shared the limited early expectations of sentence patterns. They had more difficulty, however, in remembering them, and it took them longer to learn the use of terms like *word* and *sentence* and longer to establish the knowledge of letter patterns within words and word patterns within sentences that could form the foundation for recognition across words and sentences, and so for progress through the early readers. They did not, therefore, arrive at Wilma's and John's 'take-off' points within their first two or three years in school. The reasons for this varied. Mary headed most rapidly in the desired direction, but was only just making the break when she had to change schools. It seemed that her motivation sagged most obviously in her second year when otherwise she might have carried on more successfully. Sean seemed to have some specific difficulty with visual pattern recognition. Copying complex patterns was not difficult – he was the best of the sample in this respect – and the Daniels and Diack tests confirmed this; but they also showed his weakness in recognition, confusing *b* and *d* in particular in final-letter positions. This kind of weakness had been evident from the start, and it may have been the reason for Sean's stronger attempts to gain cues from sounding to supplement the sight and meaning cues he gained from text. Dave seemed to have a different problem, that of perception of complex designs. It may have been related to a more general delay in development of ability to process information, for his use of language and his English Picture Vocabulary test score suggested this, but it made it hard for him to build a knowledge of a basic pool of known words and of English spelling from which to develop wider reading.

In spite of these differences, all three children showed certain features of skill development seen in the more successful readers. They depended on familiar contexts and visual pattern for early reading, showing by their errors that they recognised meaning and sight cues. As they made progress they were able to hazard attempts to read new words and sometimes to correct their own misreadings. They found phonic naming useful in the early stages, but were unable to use blending very much until they had made some considerable progress with the visual code and with scanning for meaning, by which time they had turned 7.

Chapter 6

The Late Beginners

While the slower learners began to show signs of learning to read in their first year at school, the remaining five children gave no such indication. They were late to begin, and had their own individual difficulties; but three shared the handicap of receiving virtually no support at home for learning to read, though this came about for different reasons. Amanda's mother frankly acknowledged and was concerned about her relative emotional and educational neglect at a difficult time in her own life. Sara had been passed from pillar to post and had experienced considerable insecurity and educational neglect. Michael's family was in straitened circumstances and he showed signs of both physical and educational neglect. Fiona and Matt, however, seemed to have support available, from their grandmother and mother respectively, but for different reasons to be unable to seek it. It was interesting that when Matt overcame some of his vision problems and his relative immaturity, and when Amanda's mother was able to be more supportive, these two children began to make progress. Their stories will be told first, followed by an account of Michael, Sara and Fiona.

MATT

Matt made a very cautious and shy start to school life, and it was difficult to assess at first how he might develop later. During his first three years he was absent more than the other children, one long absence being occasioned by an accident to his hand. He recovered well from this, only to run into difficulties with vision. Correction for a squint meant the wearing of an eye-patch and the use of drops to put his 'good eye' out of action and strengthen use of the other. Thus he was handicapped to some extent just when he was being expected to learn to read. After three years, however, when shyness and vision problems were overcome, he began to make up for his late start.

When he started school he was very small and looked younger than his age. He was very shy and most unwilling to talk to adults, and if pressed he sometimes became tearful. He was more dependent on the teacher than were most of the children and needed more help with shoes and clothes. With other children he was prepared to be friendly, but was rather timid and unable at first to fend for himself if play became somewhat rough. In his second and third years he became less withdrawn and made friends more confidently. He came from a small family, having a younger sister. His father worked as a van driver, and his mother had not been in paid employment since his birth. Her attitude to both children was very protective, and her anxiety about aggression in boys seemed to be reflected in Matt's early timidity. She was also very worried about his vision.

These points emerged during an interview with her towards the end of Matt's second year in school, when she reported that he was enjoying life there more than in his first year. He appeared to enjoy stories in school, and recounted them to her when he went home. He talked about events in the classroom and who had been in trouble and why, but he was not willing to talk about writing work or number work. He was beginning to talk about his reading and she was aware that he was looking forward to starting his next book. She knew that he could just about write his name, and judged that he could read the First Red Book, could try the Green Book, but that the Blue Book would have, as she put it, 'too much print at once'. (These judgements tallied well with what was observed at that time of his abilities in school.) She was also aware that he was not learning very quickly, and she commented that before he went to school he never seemed to read street signs or words anywhere, but only seemed to notice numbers. During the last year he had asked his mother to read to him when he did not feel very well or did not want to play out. He had not done this before he was 6. He now tried to show her his reading from the school book, which he was allowed to take home, but he did not try to read any other books to her. She had made a practice of reading to both children at night. She said that Matt had a good memory for events and talked well at home, and she did not understand his shyness with others.

Matt's own comments about his experience of reading tallied with his mother's. When interviewed about reading at 5 he said he could not yet read but that he had a 'Rupert Bear' book at home which he sometimes tried to read to his mother and father. He claimed that his mother read to him at night when he was in bed, and that both parents read the newspaper and books. He seemed to have some idea that reading yielded stories and was pleasurable. He wanted to read the Gay Way book when he was ready, but he said he did not ask anybody if he wanted help. He thought pictures helped reading, but he was unable to read anything from his folder or from the Gay Way book.

At the end of his second year in school he seemed still much less sure of the nature of reading than John and Wilma had been almost from the start. This was in spite of making some progress through the reading scheme. Like the other children he claimed to enjoy reading, but he was unable to give reasons. He liked a 'Three Bears' book at home and his Gay Way book at school. He claimed it was easy to remember words – but this may have been a relative matter, his memory now being better than earlier. He did not suggest sounding as a strategy for reading forgotten or novel words, in spite of involvement in learning such strategies. Furthermore, he did not think that sounding helped or that it always worked, and he seemed very doubtful about it. He did think pictures helped him to read, because they helped him to remember. He could give no answer to a question about the helpfulness of visual similarity. He thought reading was useful for children of his age and for older children and adults, but would give no reasons. His mother was mentioned as wanting him to learn to read, and as helping him by listening to him try. He also felt his teacher helped him. He obviously felt he was making progress with reading, and also said he would like to do more reading in school if he could.

But Matt's experience of reading had been affected by his absence and defective vision. Although his mother had provided support he had been unable to avail himself of opportunities to recognise the art of reading, apart from the experiences of listening to stories and seeing others with books and papers. He understood reading as connected with stories, and when he came to school it seemed doubtful whether he related reading and writing. The Breakthrough materials were of little immediate help to him here, for he could neither copy nor write freely any of the words he suggested for use in sentences. Writing or copying of any kind remained difficult for him, and he was usually unable to read his own writing. Improvement came in his third year in school when he was able to use both eyes freely and together. It was then that he began to be able to write a little spontaneously, although his hand was still very erratic. Had he not had defective vision, Matt's understanding of reading and writing would probably have developed faster and his abilities might have kept pace.

Although he was uncommunicative he did manage to obtain attention from his teachers and appeared to understand instructions and to follow stories with pleasure. He showed comprehension of others, though he said little enough himself. When interest and enjoyment overcame his shyness in the various tests of language use he showed no language deficiency, and his English Picture Vocabulary test score was just about the norm for his age. There was no reason to suppose, therefore, that his late start in reading was in any way caused by linguistic or general cognitive deficiency.

The handicap of defective vision became very evident in the tasks used to explore his knowledge of spelling pattern in English and the way it related to his reading, but at first he carried out tasks in much the same way as the other late beginners. In Tests A2 and A3 (Appendix A) he was willing to respond, albeit shyly, but he was unable to distinguish letters from numbers and could neither suggest nor recognise suitable examples of letters, words and sentences. The concepts seemed meaningless to him, and the task incomprehensible. He could not have been understanding the point of much of what the teacher had been saying in presenting the Breakthough approach, not even to the extent of getting some toehold that would enable him to grasp the concepts better.

Matt's prolonged absence in his first year through April until June meant that he missed the first Breakthrough test and, not surprisingly, he had no success with it in July. On returning to school he appeared rather more mature and he was a little more ready to talk. He spoke softly, but did not appear to have any articulation defect. While he could not recognise any words, or distinguish words from letters, he was willing to try, and seemed to grasp more readily what was required of him. After being shown the letter *s* he was able to find other examples in a text, and could similarly recognise *c* and *t*. He did not know these letters, either by name or sound, but he did appear to have some slight basis for beginning a visual analysis of print.

In his second year, when copying the figures in Test B1 (Appendix B) he produced firm straight lines but very uncertain curves, and he had difficulty with diagonals and with positioning gaps in the curves. In Test B2 he seemed to have difficulty identifying words – tending always to look at letters. This meant that he was unsuccessful with the first task of pointing to big and little words, but managed the letter similarity tasks better. He identified similar initial letters and initial-letter patterns quite readily, and to a limited extent saw some final two-letter patterns and a double-vowel pattern. He enjoyed the oral sentence completion task and gave good answers. The whole suggested that he was learning letter-by-letter pattern recognition, and would be able to anticipate sentence meaning in written material when he had enough initial reading skill to be in a position to employ the ability, but that his awareness of word units carrying meaning in written material was still hazy. His letter identification and matching skills were definitely stronger than at the end of the previous school year.

His classwork also showed some progress. He had obviously been willing to suggest new sentences for building, and had received the teacher's help, but his slowness in reading suggested that he did not remember them well. His writing was just about legible, and included sentences and phrases copied from his sentence-maker models and from the blackboard. He could not read them, however. Neither could he read any words in Test A5 (Appendix A), but he did possess a classroom copy of the First Red Book and read the first page correctly. He was able to point to each word afterwards and give a correct reading of each, although he was asked to do so in a fairly random order. His only error was to point to *The* for both *lorry* and *The*. It seemed, then, that he not only knew what the 'message' of that page was, but that he connected it with word meaning. On the second page he began to read *The pots and pans went up the hill in the lorry* as *The red lorry . . .* and then abandoned it, his knowledge of individual words on the first page not yet generalising to the second. His classwork in his writing and number books had not developed much further by mid-November; but he showed signs of beginning to recognise what he had written. If cued with the first word or with his own drawing he could remember a whole sentence. He could correctly read figures in his number work book, but not words. His writing (copying) was poorly formed and erratic and included the inversion *b* for *d*.

It was surprising, then, that in the same month Matt seemed to make significant steps forward with his reading. In the First Red Book he had read the first three pages with the teacher, and when his reading was sampled he managed the following extracts from those and from three further pages. He was then 5 years 7 months old.

Extracts from the First Red Book (Gay Way)
The big red lorry went up the hill. The pots and pans went up the hill in the lorry. Up and up to the top went the big red lorry. Up and up and up went the pots. Up went the pans.

 It went down the hill.

Up and on and on and up went the big red lorry.

Deb the little rat went down the hill.

The first extracts were read steadily, the only errors being confusion of *pots* and *pans* three times. When asked to read each misread word again Matt did so without error. In the further extract he failed to read *It went*, but did read *down the hill* before he was told the first two words. He read the next extracts completely except for *Deb*, which he was then told. This reading was quite impressive, given that he had not reached with his teacher the pages from which the second and subsequent extracts were taken. He was able to recognise in new contexts the words he had learned from the earliest pages and from support work with cards in class. He was not reading new words, but old words in new contexts. This suggested a grasp of an important aspect of reading, but no grasp of word decoding.

Some further signs of improvement in reading were noticed in February.

Extract from the First Red Book (Gay Way)
Sam the red fox ran down the hill. Sam had no house to live in. Bang, bang, ting, ting, went Sam on the tin house.

Matt's reading (Age 5 years 10 months)
Sam* the red fox (red) ran* d-?-n, D-ow*-n, down* the hill. Sam had* (on) no* house to live in. Bang, bang, ting, ting, w-e-n-t, went* Sam on* the tin house.

Matt was still reading from memory of individual words, and quite smoothly from familiar phrases, but signs of decoding strategies were emerging. All the asterisked words had to be supplied because he could not recall them in this context, but his misreading of *ran* showed the influence of internal visual similarity between words, and his attempt to sound *down* revealed an awareness of the possibility of cueing from letter–sound correspondence, derived from phonic naming of letters.

Yet further steps in learning to read were apparent in this sampling in May.

Extract from the First Red Book (Gay Way)
Deb the rat and Ben the dog ran up, up, up the hill. Sam the fox ran, ran, ran to the top of the hill. The fat pig went down, down, down the hill. No little tin pot house to live in. No hen and no cat. No red fox and no dog. No little rat. No fat pig.

Matt's reading (Age 6 years 1 month)
Deb the (little) rat and Ben the dog ran up, up, up the hill. Sam the fox ran, ran, ran to the (pot) t-o-p, top of the hill. The fat pig

went down, down, down the hill. N-o, no* little tin pot house to l*-i-v-e, live* in. No h*-e-n, hen* and (on) no cat. No red fox and no dog. No little (ran) r-a-t*, rat*. No fat pig.

Matt was still reading word by word, but with intonation and with some smoothness in phrases. His addition of *little* to the first sentence was due to his familiarity with the phrase *Deb the little rat.* His other errors showed graphic similarity between the word and its misreading, as in *pot* for *top*, *on* for *no* and *ran* for *rat*. In the case of *no* he corrected himself, presumably being guided by the sense, but with the other two he needed encouragement to sound them and was then successful with *top* and with *rat* when helped with blending the sounds. He was uncertain, however, of the sounds to associate with some of the letters, and had to be helped with *l*, *h*, *t* and *o* (long).

When seen in class in November in his third year he was not working with the Sound Sense books, as were most of the other children, but was copying from a story-book in order to improve his writing. This was not at all strong. He was able to copy a few words reasonably well but then his writing deteriorated to a spidery, erratic, indecipherable scribble. This pattern of performance was evident for several pieces of work in his writing-book, and it seemed that his vision, limited while one eye was being treated, was not adequate to sustain much copying or writing.

When reading he held his book very close to his eyes, and was effectively able to use only one eye. Nevertheless, he wished to read and the following transcript was made. He was attempting to read from the Second Red Book (age 6 years 7 months).

You are* little. You can get in, Deb, and live in the old shoe house. So (Ben) Deb the little rat, Jip the cat and Ben the dog l-i-v-e-d, lived* in the old shoe house on the hill.
Meg the hen went up the hill. She went and sat on top of the old red lorry. She jumped down* and (run) ran, ran, ran to the old shoe on the hill.
It is a house. It is the old shoe house. Who lives in it? Ting, ting, ting, ting. I will get in.

Matt read more smoothly than on previous occasions, and with intonation. He needed help with the asterisked words, but corrected his other two errors himself.

His reading until now had given little evidence of the graphic similarity errors seen in the other children's attempts, and it seemed likely that he was depending very much on letter-by-letter rather than letter pattern strategies of remembering and of attempting words. This being so it seemed unlikely that he had acquired much knowledge of the patterning of English spelling, and it was not surprising to find that his sorting of words in Tests C1 and C2 (Appendix C) was random with respect to their status as true, nonsense, or non-English words. He quite liked the idea of there being some 'foreign' words in the pack, and he enjoyed sorting the cards, but the basis of his sorting was not discernible. He was also keen to try the *e*-cancelling task at which he worked systematically, cancelling each line in turn from left to right. He deleted well over half of the *e*s, mostly missing those in mid-positions, and deleted no other letters. This revealed some conformity to the mechanics of reading and writing, sufficient visual acuity and discrimination to perform the task, and some idea of which parts of words he attended to most readily. The suggestion of some regularity in word perception promised future development of letter pattern perception.

By February in his third year he spoke of finding it hard to read from the blackboard and from other books, so that his work in class was generally rather limited by his lack of reading ability. Nevertheless, his vision had improved under treatment so that he was able to use both eyes together. He was still working from the Red Books, as indicated in the transcript below (age 6 years 10 months).

I d-o-n-t, dont* k-n-o-w, know* (went) what to do said the old woman. (Will you) We will come with you to look for a (pig) big house, said Sam and the fat pig. So the old woman, the children, Sam and the fat pig went on t-i-ll, till* they came to the shoe house.
(This) It is too old and too little. (Will) We will go on, said Sam.

He spontaneously tried sounding words when he did not recognise them, but he needed help. Some errors were misreadings based on incorrect expectations, and these usually showed some graphic similarity with the correct version. Again, when Matt could read a sequence without having to stop he did so with some phrasing and intonation.

His score on the basic Daniels and Diack test was very low, since he was only able to read five of the short questions, but he managed to copy the abstract figures rather more accurately than Dave had done, and his work was neat. Similarly, his sentence copying was neat and accurate, but he failed to space the words. His visual discrimination and orientation performance was good, so it seemed that he had some perceptual difficulty of a similar nature to Dave's, though in Matt's case it might well have been due to inadequate learning because of vision difficulties. His aural discrimination was good, but he was not very good at letter recognition, especially at the ends of words. He found the diagnostic word recognition tests very difficult. In the first, the easiest, he made errors of a graphic similarity kind, for example, *ton* for *ten*, *and* for *had* and *cat* for *cut*. With the harder items he failed to show any consonant-blending skill or knowledge of digraphs, and he reduced polysyllabic words to single syllables. All in all, he was able to try sounding letter by letter, but not able to do much else. In the oral and picture word recognition tests he made several errors, but he chose items which were most similar to those desired. This suggested the early stages of graphic pattern appreciation. Interpreting these tests left one with the conclusion that his reading depended very much on some well-learned cues to familiar word recognition and on the sense of what he was reading.

By the summer term his reading had improved further, and he was reading from the First Blue Book (age 7 years 2 months).

> A robin lost six eggs out of her nest. So she went to Ben the dog. Did you take six eggs out of my nest? Yap, yap, yap. I did not. I gave you a bit of my coat to put in your nest. But I did not take the eggs away.

In spite of an error-free reading he was still tending to produce a mixture of word-by-word reading together with some phrasing. He read at an even pace, with some intonation, and with a card to mark his line. His comprehension of what he had been reading was perfectly adequate.

The end of his third year in school saw Matt about two years behind the norm in reading ability. His performance was something like Wilma's and John's at the end of their first year. How far and how quickly his improved vision would enable him to reduce the gap remained to be seen.

AMANDA

Amanda was relatively slightly built, but generally healthy and with no apparent vision or hearing problems. Her school attendance was good. While it was difficult to pinpoint the basis of the observation, she seemed at first slightly unusual, if not a little strange, in her behaviour with other children. She was not unkind or aggressive, but rather jerky and variable in her responses. She also showed signs of deliberate withdrawal from situations, including the general teaching sessions in the classroom. She could be present in body but absent in mind. Occasionally she could be surprisingly stubborn in a quiet way. In her second year at school some of these characteristics began to fade, and she made friends with other children. She was the elder of two sisters who lived with their mother, the parents having separated. Towards the end of Amanda's second year in school, when she was 6 years old, her mother remarried; and this change in home circumstances led to a decision to transfer her to another school.

Before this it was possible to obtain an interview with her mother, who reported that Amanda did not talk much about schoolwork, but that she felt that she was getting better at reading and that she enjoyed stories at school. She did talk about her school friends, dinners, assembly in the hall and songs that she had sung. In fact she enjoyed singing very much. When talking about Amanda's learning to read her mother commented that she had no books at home, no comics and no crayoning-books. She had asked her mother to read to her, but the latter preferred to tell stories that she herself invented. She said she used to read to Amanda when she was 4 years old and at present did so to a younger sister, but having said this she then revealed that she could not actually read herself. What she meant by reading to the children was that she held a book open on her knee, and told a story. She nevertheless had a realistic assessment of Amanda's own skills. She knew she could write her name and she judged she would find the First Red Book hard. She knew that Amanda was relatively slow at learning to read, and she went on to blame herself for it, not, as one might expect, because she had reading difficulties herself, but because her own personal problems had in her view led her to neglect the children. She was hoping for a new start with her second marriage and an anticipated new baby. In spite of the air of optimism, however, it was clear that Amanda was going to have to make further adjustments to new situations, both at home and school, while learning to read.

Amanda's own accounts of reading revealed the way a severe initial lack of understanding gave way to greater comprehension as she approached 7. When she was just 5 she could say nothing about the wall display of Breakthrough words though she was aware that television was connected with it in some way. In Test A2 (Appendix A) she showed no idea of numbers, letters, words, or sentences. When asked about aspects of reading she was inclined to withdraw. Sometimes she simply looked away completely as though her mind was elsewhere. Indeed she actually gave the impression that she was looking at another person although there was none there. When her attention was recalled she was inclined to nod as a response so that no real weight could be given to her assent. When she volunteered information she seemed to conceive of reading as looking at a book, and said she had a 'party' book at home and that her mother read to her.

A month later she said she could now read, claiming to read names and saying she wanted to read a book. She had a classwork writing-book which she offered to read. The simple sentence *I am Ben the dog* was all it contained, but she could not read it in spite of her willingness to co-operate. She was quite able to repeat the spoken sentence, but entirely unable to reproduce it when looking at the written form. Even after three demonstrations and word-by-word reading with pointing, she was unable to read it as a complete sentence. She did not keep her eyes fixed on each word, nor even on the sentence. Even in the trial runs she kept looking away in a restless manner. When asked what she would do if she did not know a word she said she would ask Sara, who was then her friend, but who would be a most unlikely source of help with reading. She would not ask the teacher.

Since she could make no attempt at reading by the end of her first year, a conversation about the Breakthrough materials was recorded instead. She was able to recognise examples of the letters *s*, *c*, *a* and *t*, being able to name the first two phonically, though she indicated the letters in response to being asked if she knew any of the words, and still seemed unable to use the terms *letter* and *word* meaningfully. She said again that she would ask Sara for help if she needed it, but this time she also said she would ask her teacher and her younger sister (aged 3). She said she could not remember words or letters, but that she thought she would be able to read when she was 6. She did not seem to think she need try now. She had obviously found reading an incomprehensible exercise during her first year, and had not brought any skills to bear on the understanding of print. She seemed scarcely able to attend sufficiently to make a beginning.

During her second year Amanda began to work with the Gay Way book, although she had little understanding of reading. In November she offered to read from the First Red Book. She 'read' the first page nearly correctly as *The (big) red lorry went up the hill*, but when asked to point to *red* she pointed to a patch of red colour in the picture, and when asked to read the print again read *Up the red lorry went up the hill*. The next page was read as *The red went down the hill*. She was reading the picture rather than the text and remembering as well as she could what formula to use. She produced it in a curiously stilted, one-word-at-a-time fashion, in spite of not being able to identify each word.

From this point on she painstakingly tried to learn the right thing to say when confronted with her book, and worked slowly through the first few pages during the rest of the year. At the end of this time she claimed to like reading a lot, but qualified this by saying she got fed up sometimes. She said she liked a 'Snow White' book at home and her Gay Way book at school. She admitted to difficulty in remembering words, but said she used sounding to read words she had forgotten. On the other hand, she said she would leave a new word alone. She thought sounding always helped, as it possibly did in the context of recall; she also thought pictures helped her reading because they showed what was happening, and she thought reading was useful at all ages but could give no reasons. She said her mother wanted her to learn to read, and helped her by reading to her and listening to her reading at bed-time. She did not want to spend more time reading in school, but would prefer painting.

Her third year was spent in another school. The following report was given by the headteacher after she had spent a year in her new setting.

Amanda transferred to this school shortly before Christmas a year ago.

When she came she recognised few words, and did her writing by copying sentences that the teacher had already written out. During last year she appeared to make good progress. She was writing interesting stories although she usually needed to translate them and had sometimes forgotten what she had written.

Amanda has settled down well within the school, although she is still lacking in self-confidence. Her work is below average, and a September Screening Test [Young's] showed her to have a reading quotient of 88. She attended remedial classes for a while, as a border-line case, but was found to be more able than the other children within the group and therefore is now working in the class on the Oxford Junior Workbooks (OUP). She is on Book 1.

On arrival at this school Amanda was put on to 'Through the Rainbow' reading scheme, Red Book 1, and has now progressed to Blue Book 2. She is now beginning to read with more fluency and understanding, although her reading level is still not really adequate for the work generally undertaken by the class. Spelling is poor and general sentence construction needs a lot of working on.

This was entirely consistent with the story of the first two years, but was rather encouraging. Amanda's general ability was never assessed, but it seemed likely that her whole performance in school was clouded by the difficulties at home and by her own bewilderment about reading. Unfortunately she seemed to find no enlightenment through trying to write, for the Breakthrough approach made no link with her understanding of reading as something to do with books and stories. She was able to copy reasonably well, but seemed to have no concept of communicating through writing until she grasped that the text carried the stories in books. Although she suggested sentences to the teacher, and tried to copy the string of words built by her from the Breakthrough cards, she failed to identify these cards as having anything to do with what she had said and was therefore unable to 'read' them.

The first signs of learning which might form the foundation for some knowledge of English orthography came in her second year. Her copying of figures in Test B1 (Appendix B) was much more successful than that of the previous year. The geometric figures were much firmer and better arranged, and her treatment of diagonals was far better. The letters were copied rather less firmly, with very tentative vertical lines, but with correct orientation. Her name was written very untidily, with a reversal of n, but with an initial capital. In Test B2 she did better than in earlier tasks, but she was not at all certain about the first item. She pointed to letters rather than words in response to the requests to indicate little and big words. This uncertainty about identifying words had persisted for over a year and she was not yet reading simple sentences. In the second item she was able to recognise and match the letters s, e and h; in the third she could match the initial pairs sl, th and ch, though she took a little time to grasp the task; in the fourth she was only able to match single final letters, though in the fifth she not only matched the double centre letters oo and ee, but saw the double letters tt in a word on the same page. Her oral sentence completion was good.

By November in her second year she had copied a few sentences in her writing-book, but errors included reversals of s, n and a, and a p for a d and a reversed n for m. She could not read sentences she had written – sentences like *I like my mum*, *I like television* and *I am at school*. Although she could count correctly up to ten, she could not read figures she had written in her number-book. Two weeks after her first reading from the First Red Book a further sampling was obtained. This time she read *The big red lorry went up the hill* as *The big red hen went up the hill*; and from *The pots and pans went up the hill in the lorry* she recognised *The* and, when supplied with *pots*, went on to read *and pans*, stalled at *went*, but then went on to read *up the hill in the lorry*. She could not attempt any further reading, but she did seem to be attending more usefully to the text in spite of her heavy dependence on attempted recall.

In December her reading of the First Red Book was again sampled. She now showed signs of self-correction as indicated by the brackets below.

Amanda's reading (Age 5 years 9 months)
The big red (went) lorry went up the hill. The (red) p-, (pans and pots) pots and pans* (the) went* up the hill in* the (pots) (pans) lorry.

This shows a still tenuous hold on remembering the words, but in addition to trying to match her reading to the print she was now able to correct herself. Where this was not achieved the correct reading was supplied as in *pots and pans* for *pans and pots*, *went* for *the*, and *in* where no reading was offered. Her attempt to sound *pots* by reading *p* was abortive, but it was an indication that she was aware of possibilities in this direction.

The following sample of reading was recorded in February:

Extract from the First Red Book (Gay Way)
Bang, bang, bang, bang. Ting, ting, ting, ting. A tin pot fell down. It fell down on the hill. It went down the hill.

Amanda's reading (Age 5 years 11 months)
Ting, ting, ting, ting*. Ting, ting, ting, ting. A (pot) tin* pot* fell* (on) down*. It* fell down on the hill. It* went* down (on) the hill.

She was not aware of her misreading of the *Bang* sequence and, until she had been helped to see it, did not recognise the difference between the two sequences. She began to read the first real sentence, but misread *tin* and could make no suggestion for the rest except *on* for *down*. Here there seemed to be tendencies to recognise similar aspects of the graphic appearance of words, and to misread accordingly. When the complete sentence was supplied Amanda was asked to read it until she was word-perfect. She needed six attempts before she was successful, but then she seemed able to maintain the reading. Apart from the need to be told *It* she read the next sentence without error; but in the last she needed to be told *It* again, she had forgotten *went* and she misread *the* because she carried forward the phrasing of the previous sentence. She was, however, able to correct herself. She was delighted with her effort, and it was interesting to observe the way her initial anxieties had been soothed as she was helped through the task.

By the summer her writing was improving. She was able to write her name, spelling it correctly, but reversing one letter. Her handwriting was firm, and the letters were well formed in both free and copied writing. She copied sentences without error, except the omission of letters from *robin lost* to give *rost*, but she needed much encouragement and approval to continue. Approval, in fact, resulted in a marked increase in willingness to do the task. For the dictated sentence *I went in the lorry* she would only manage *I wi . . . i . . .* and for her own suggestion she tried *I am a mum* (a sentence used in classwork), but only managed *Iy nuny*.

Another reading was sampled in June.

Extract from the First Red Book (Gay Way)
So the fat pig sat on the top of the little tin pot house.
Fat pig sat on and on. Fat pig sat and sat and sat.

Amanda's reading (Age 6 years 3 months)
So the fat pig (a) s-at, sat* on the (tin pot house) (t-o-m) t-o-p, top* of the little tin pot house. F-a-t, Fat pig sat on (a) a-n-d, and* on. Fat pig sat and sat and sat.

She now had a firmer memory of words she had come across before, and was beginning to tackle new words by sounding them, but except for *fat* she needed help in blending the sounds, as indicated by the asterisks. Her misreading of *top* was a mixture of a tendency to read a phrase already met elsewhere and recognition of a visual similarity between *tin* and *top*. Again she seemed to need much encouragement to keep going, but was pleased at the end.

In this tentative move towards reading Amanda was showing a similar sequence of development to that displayed by the other children. Once it was possible to attempt recall of several sentences drawn from a common pool of words, there were signs of some unconscious recognition of the patterning of spelling in that pool. More was happening than letter-by-letter and word-by-word identification.

MICHAEL

Michael was rather small in build, and did not appear to be cared for as well as most of the other children. He looked less clean and tidy, and often seemed to have a slight cold. At a medical examination when he was 5 he was found to require glasses, he was left-handed, and he was judged to need speech therapy for an articulation problem. During his third term in his first year at school he had to spend some days in hospital for an eye operation. His attendance at school was quite good, in spite of these difficulties. He was the youngest of a family of four children with neither parent working; both were at home, and the paternal grandfather also lived with them. He was not shy – on the contrary, he approached both children and adults – but his speech was so difficult to understand that he met considerable discouragement. During his first two years in school speech therapy, and possibly also his school experience, improved his articulation considerably. A combination of personal handicap and social disadvantage contributed to his slow learning. It was not possible to obtain an interview with his mother to fill out the information about his background, but Michael's own comments suggested that he received very little, if any, support for learning to read.

He reported that his father read the paper and his mother read comics, and he could refer to no book at home except for a note-book and the Gay Way book the teacher allowed him to take with him. He thought pictures helped reading, but any reference to story reading at home produced very confused and uncertain replies. Even at 7 he could only refer to a few books in school, and his reading amounted to little more than recalling a few words. By then he claimed to find it easy to remember words, but this may simply have reflected a feeling that his limited success at this stage was better than his previous state. He suggested sounding letters to try forgotten and novel words, and thought it always helped. He thought pictures helped, too, but could not give a reason. He judged reading to be useful for his age-group and for older children who could read better, but he was unable to give a view about adults. He did not think anyone helped him to read at home or school, not even the teacher, but he said he would like to read more in school if he could. Altogether his comments suggested a better understanding than at 5 of the nature of reading and of the technical terms involved in talking about it.

Unlike the other children Michael was handicapped by a language problem – his articulation defect. He did not use plural endings when he started school, and he dropped all consonant word-endings. He retained the correct number of syllables, but some of his words seemed more characteristic of the 2-year-old, as with *kaka* for *carrot*, *bika* for *biscuit*, *mikter* for *mister* and *da* for *that*. He seemed able, however, to produce most consonant sounds provided that they occurred in the first position. This defect made it difficult for him to be understood by his teachers and to show that he had read words correctly. Since he appeared to have no auditory perception loss, however, it was a moot point whether the articulation loss of detail affected his learning to read in any more fundamental way. It was certain, however, that his absences for eye treatment and his propensity for losing his spectacles contributed to his difficulties and delay. Moreover, although it was never clear that he suffered any purely linguistic handicap, his vocabulary score was well below the norm for his age, and his answers to some of the tasks exploring language abilities were more confused than those of the other children mentioned so far. His delay in learning to read may therefore have been part of a more general slowness in learning.

Although he was willing to attempt to read, it was clear from the start that Michael had much to learn of the perception of pattern in text. He knew about units such as letters, words and sentences, but nothing about questions of their arrangement. When he was 5 his pattern copying was very erratic, but he copied individual letters in a more or less recognisable way. He had the words *I*, *am*, *at* and *school* in his sentence-maker, and he could sometimes build the corresponding sentence. Once he arranged them as *school am I at* and read them as *I am the television*. When asked to point to *I* and *am* he did so correctly. The words were then rearranged to form *I am at school* and Michael was reminded of the reading. It was then rearranged to *am I at school*, which he judged to be a sentence but which he read as *I am at school*. He did the same for *at am school I*, and yet was able to point correctly to each word. It seemed that he had not grasped the importance of word order in sentences.

When given the Breakthrough test in April Michael could only read *I* and did not attempt any other words. He fared no better with the sentences, and when retested a month or two later, after his eye operation and absence, he failed to read anything. In answer to requests to read words he volunteered knowledge of some of the letters, sounding them as he went. He identified examples of *m*, *s*, *a*, *c* and *e*; and, when asked, he could find other examples of each. His attention in reading seemed to have moved entirely away from words and sentences to the visual and phonetic identification of letters, as though at each testing he was responding in line with recent work in school, but failing to build on his earlier knowledge.

At the beginning of his second year he copied the figures in Test B1 (Appendix B) with difficulty. Orientation of diagonals and the positioning of gaps in curved figures caused most problems. His copying of his own name (he could not attempt it without a model) was extraordinary. It was a complete reversal of the names, writing from right to left, but with no apparent letter reversals, though each letter was formed in a very erratic manner. Michael was left-handed, and this may well have led to his choice not to write from left to right, but it would not necessarily have led to his transformation of letter order. This implied a learning to read the letters in order from left to right, and then a complete reordering from right to left in the process of writing.

In Test B2 (Appendix B) he showed himself to be still uncertain about the term *word*. He pointed to individual letters and sounded them when asked to indicate big and little words. His letter matching was quite good, however, and again he sounded those he chose to indicate. He took to the third item easily and saw the patterns *sl* and *ch* quite readily. More surprisingly, considering his difficulties in the previous year, he found the final-letter pattern matching in the fourth item possible at the two-letter level, and he had no trouble matching the central *oo* and *ee* in the fifth item. His oral sentence completion was quite good, though his articulation of *sleep* for *We —— in a bed* was so poor that there was some uncertainty about the word.

Michael's classwork had given him twelve words in his sentence-maker rather than the four, *I*, *am*, *at* and *school*, previously observed. Additional words were *cat*, *the*, *me*, *see*, *like*, *dog* and *Jip*. There was also a full stop. He had evidently experimented with various sentences based on the verbs *am*, *see* and *like*. His writing was very erratic, however, for he copied phrases with very great difficulty over the shape and order of letters. He read no words in Test A5 (Appendix A), but did have a school reader – the First Red Book. He read the first page, *The big red lorry went up the hill*, as *Red lorry went up to the hill*, and the second, *The pots and pans went up the hill in the lorry*, as *Pan and tin, red lorry*. In both cases he pointed very vaguely to the whole page and when asked to re-read the former, pointing to the words, he could not do it. What appeared to happen was that the picture and general appearance of the page cued him to remembering some of the sense of the associated print. He did, however, connect sense with the array of words, not just with the picture. His classwork books showed that he had been trying to develop his copying and to build a store of sentences. One of his own invention was *My monster is upside down*, and his teacher had given him an accurate model to read and copy. He could not read it, however, nor could he read any of his own writing. His only correct 'reading', *I like my baby*, was marred by his using the same offering as a reading for another sentence. He simply knew it was there somewhere! His copying was very erratic and full of reversal errors, though not of letter order error. Many letters were very poorly formed.

In February he was trying to read from the First Red Book, but with great difficulty, as shown below.

Extract from the First Red Book (Gay Way)
Ben the dog ran to the top of the hill. He ran up to the old red lorry.

Michael's reading (Age 5 years 10 months)
Ben the dog (little) r-a*, (rat) r-a-n*, ran (on) to* the (t-o-b) t-o-p*, top of the hill. He* (had) (rat) r-a-n*, ran up (on) to* the old* (shoe) red lorry.

His reading of *little* for *ran* was inexplicable, but when asked to try sounding he was able to blend sounds to read the word. The same was true of *top*, where the reading of *b* for *p* was of interest, but all other errors were corrected by supplying the correct reading for him. His errors showed the use of various cues, visual similarity in *rat* for *ran*, in *ran* and *had* for *rat*, and in *on* for *to*, phonic help in *ran* and *top*, and familiar sense in *the old shoe* for *the old red lorry*.

By the third term Michael's writing was becoming clearer and more regular, but he wrote his name less confidently then he copied, and not without letter order error. He copied some sentences without any mistakes, however, though he failed to space words properly. He wrote with his left hand, but kept to left–right order. He sounded each letter as he copied, and he completed the set task. When asked to write *I went in the lorry* he managed *I . . . ir . . . r . . .*, leaving a space for *went*, failing with *n* in *in*, and recalling no more than *r* for *lorry*. He suggested *My mum is kind* (a sentence he had met in school) as something he might write, but he could manage nothing of it.

A further attempt at reading from the First Red Book was sampled in May.

Extract from the First Red Book (Gay Way)
Bang, bang, bang, bang. Ting, ting, ting, ting. Who is it? It is the fat pig. Who are you? I am fat pig.

Michael's reading (Age 6 years 1 month)
(The fat pig) B-a-n-g, bang, b-a-n-g, bang, bang, bang. (went) T-i-n-g, ting, ting, ting. W-h-o, who* (are) i-s-, is i-t, it? I, I-t, It i-s, is a f-a-t, (tin) fat* pig. W-h-o, Who are you? I am (the) fat pig.

Michael began by identifying the fat pig as the focus of the reading, either from memory of aspects of the text or, more probably, from the accompanying picture. He started sounding the *Bang* sequence, and was successful. The same happened for the *Ting* group. In the subsequent four sentences he sounded most of the words, and succeeded with those not asterisked. For these he needed help. Certain errors such as *are* for *is* and *the* for *fat* seemed to be anticipatory errors based on earlier reading. In spite of the slow progress the reading showed some signs of development of skill.

Although he was attempting to use the first Sound Sense exercise-book when observed in class in November, some of his letters were reversed in his writing. Nevertheless, he seemed to understand the nature of the task of finding words with an *i*, and his word spacing was good. At this time he should have been wearing glasses all the time, but he often mislaid them or reported them broken. He had moved on from the First Red Book to the Second, and a transcript of his reading, without glasses, went as follows (age 6 years 7 months).

I am (Ben) Deb* the l-i-t-t-l-e, likkle* (ran) r-a-t, rat.
I w-e-n-t, went* t-i-n-g, ting* ting, ting. I w-i-l-l, will* g-e-t, get (the) in.
(Cat) Can* I live in the (tin, house) shoe.* I (house) ha-v-e, have* no house to live in.

Michael was keen to try reading this, but obviously read with difficulty, for he needed help with all the asterisked words. He was able to sound individual letters, but almost always unable to meld them into a word. Only with *rat* and *get* was he successful in this approach, but he picked the words up very quickly when his own jerky sounding was repeated back to him more smoothly. His ear for the words seemed to be good enough.

He did not seem able to understand Test C1 (Appendix C), but did try C2 because he wanted to have a turn like the others. His sorting of words into English and non-English seemed to favour familiar true words over others, but this may have been a chance outcome, for his reading ability seemed too poor to give him any real basis for sorting. He also tried the *e*-cancelling task, where he was moderately successful, deleting just over half the *e*s and no other letters. He explored the text rather erratically, however, treating three or four lines at a time as a block, and his pattern of cancelling bore little relation to any graphic or phonic distributional significance, except possibly a tendency to notice more initial than other positions.

His speech had improved very considerably by this third year, and he was both quick and polite in it. He had no support at home for his reading, however, not even claiming to have a comic to look at. He recognised that he could not do quite a number of things in lessons, because he could not read well enough; but he was persevering with the reading. The following is taken from a sample from the Fifth Red Book (age 6 years 10 months).

> No, old w-o-m-a-n, woman*. (We, will) We (are in the old house) live in the new house w-i-t-n, with* Meg the hen, (little rat) Deb the rat, Sam the fox and (red pig) the fat pig.

This was a short, but very serious, attempt. He was carried on by his own impetus into his expectations rather than readings. When halted he tried sounding, but, although able to sound individual letters, was still not able to smooth them into words and had to be helped. The misreading of *n* for *h* suggested that his letter knowledge might be somewhat uncertain.

He was unable to read the items in the Daniels and Diack test, and his copying of complex figures was very inaccurate, though moderately neat. His sentence copying was accurate enough, but his word spacing was unsure and his lettering rather untidy. Thus he seemed to suffer a difficulty with complex perceptual grasp similar to that shown by Dave and Matt. He also made an error or two in the visual discrimination and orientation test, but none in the aural test. He was able to identify initial but not final letters in words. This tallied with his *e*-cancelling performance. He had great difficulty with the diagnostic word recognition tests, and even in the simple ones made errors such as *is* for *if*, *cat* for *cut*, *kin* for *kit* and *with* for *win*. He was unable to blend consonants and could not face more difficult items. In short words and nonsense syllables designed to test reversals he sounded individual letters and could not read the words, but he did not misread any letters as reversals, he simply did not know them very well. In the oral and picture word recognition tests he enjoyed the task of pointing to appropriate words, and made fewer errors. Moreover, his wrong selections were usually words graphically most similar to the correct version. It was as though he had some perception of the letter patterns to be associated with spoken or mentally rehearsed words.

SARA

Sara was a small, slightly built, pale child, who was at first so shy that she seemed fearful of a stranger. She tended to adopt a withdrawing posture when approached, and to lower her head in such a way that she glanced slightly sideways and upwards from under her hair to see what was happening. She was very quiet in class, but did mix with other children in play as the first year passed, and by the time she was 6 years old she was settling well. Her attendance at school was very good, and she appeared to have no vision or hearing defects. Her home background, however, was very unsettled, and this led to disruption in her schooling. When she started school she was living with her grandmother, with her older brother and with two younger step-sisters. Some of the grandmother's own younger children were still at home, and the house was overcrowded. Sara's mother and step-father were living elsewhere in the city. When she was 6 years old her mother decided that she would like the children with her, so they left the grandmother's house to join their parents. This meant a change of school, yet within the year the children were back with their grandmother and returning to the original school. It seemed probable that the unsettled background contributed to Sara's slow learning in school, but it was impossible to obtain an interview with her mother or grandmother to try to fill out the picture.

When first approached in school she was too shy to say anything at all, but she gradually thawed as the year progressed and it became possible to assess her general language and cognitive abilities. It became clear that she had no articulation defects, though she spoke with the characteristic dialect of the district and, like the other children, showed some of the immaturities of the average 5-year-old. She could also sustain conversation, both with other children and with adults, but was not observed doing so very much until her second year in school. The two most obvious deficiencies in her use of language were inability to express a story theme and conceptual confusion in the various tasks outlined in Test B5 (Appendix B). She was able to follow instructions, and to join in with interest and make suggestions, but her explanations and comments were often only vaguely linked to the task in hand. This vagueness and confusion characterised much of her experience in school, and it was hardly surprising to find it in her understanding of reading and writing.

Early in her first year she spoke of reading as people looking at books quietly, by themselves. She spoke of her father reading the paper, though who she meant was never clear, and claimed she had a book 'with birds' at home. She described it as new, with pictures and letters in it, and said that her mother bought her books as well as shoes, and helped her to look at them. What she meant by books was obscure, and any interest shown by her parents must have been restricted to times when they visited. She had no idea of the use of the terms *number*, *letter*, *word* and *sentence*, making random guesses and irrelevant suggestions in Tests A2 and A3 (Appendix A).

Her classwork was progressing very slowly. She found some difficulty in copying letters and many of her attempts had a letter-like appearance but were unrecognisable. She attempted to copy her name, achieving the correct number of symbols, but with very little success with each. She had a personal Breakthrough folder by early March with the words for the sentence *I am at school*, which she could build correctly. When talking about reading then she said she could not yet read and did not want to learn. She again referred to her parents reading books and the newspapers; and she claimed her grandmother read stories to her nearly every night, and that she sometimes tried to read to her grandmother, but she seemed to be thinking of telling and talking rather than reading. She thought that pictures helped reading; but she was unable, or unwilling, to read her folder sentence. It seemed as though her references to reading were best interpreted as 'looking at, and talking about'. She did not respond to questions about likenesses between words and resisted attempts to explore her visual and phonic skills. Her resistance took the form of withdrawal of attention, a tendency to curl up into a ball on her chair, a refusal to look at either the materials or the interviewer and a refusal to speak. The strategy was similar to her actions when shy.

In April she was unable to read any of the words on the Break-through sheet and she again failed to do so in June. By the end of the school year, in July, she was willing to try to read from a Break-through reader *My mum*. The first page, with a facing picture, contained only these two words, which Sara read correctly. The second page, again illustrated, contained *My mum is big*, which Sara read as *My mum is bigger*, and the third page had *My mum is pretty*, which Sara read correctly. She could read no more. On exploring her reading it transpired that the only word she could correctly identify was *mum*. She could not point to *My* in the first sentence, nor to *My*, *is* or *bigger* (*big*) in the second. Yet when the observer pointed to *is* on the second page and asked Sara to find another word like it she correctly located *is* on the third page. She was able therefore to begin to identify a letter pattern, but she did not associate the written words on the page with their spoken form in a one-to-one manner. She attempted to match the written phrase to the spoken phrase. She said that she found it hard to remember the words; and she knew about sounding letters because it was done in class, but she was unable to give appropriate sounds for letters and she did not attempt such an approach herself. When asked who she would turn to for help in finding what a word said, she said she would ask one of her aunts who lived at home (one of her grand-mother's younger children). She also said she would look for this aunt in another classroom if she wanted help in school – yet no aunt was in this particular school at the time. She seemed to be rather confused about school, apart from what happened in her own class, and not clear about her own family. She said she would not ask her teacher for help, and it seemed possible that she had not yet connected her classroom activities with what little she understood of reading.

One of her conceptual confusions became evident during her second year, when she was observed playing 'Guess the word' with a group of girls who were taking turns to draw a Breakthrough word card out of a bag of such cards. She quite obviously thought that to say any word in association with any card was all that was required. The idea that a written word had a single corresponding spoken version had not taken hold, and written words had as yet no symbolic function for her. At the most she recognised the naming function of *Mum* and *Sara*. She had thus been unable to make any use of the Breakthrough or Gay Way materials, being bewildered by all tasks except for copying. She did this dutifully with slowly developing skill, but with no understanding that it had anything to do with reading. Writing was a complete mystery.

How she attempted to meet school requirements in her second year in spite of her confusion is traced in part in the next page or two. In most situations she was much less shy and it was easier to attempt to assess her skills and abilities. She copied the figures in Test B1 (Appendix B) with difficulty in drawing diagonals and in positioning gaps in curved shapes. She copied all the letters as *p*. In Test B2 she could sort little and big words and could match some single letters, naming them phonically. She took some time to grasp the third item, but then managed to match for both *ch* and *th*. In the final letter matching she could only manage single letters, but she recognised *oo* and *ee* patterns. Her oral sentence completion was not good. She offered no suggestions for omissions within sentences, and did not manage to complete all the examples with final-word omissions. This failure suggested that, even if she could manage the graphic and phonic skills needed in early sentence reading, she might have difficulty relating words in sentences that were abstracted from a context of everyday use.

In classwork at this time she was making very little perceptible progress with her writing and reading. She had only nine words in her Breakthrough folder – a measure of her lack of suggestions for sentence building, combined with her difficulty in memorising words. Her writing and number booklets contained attempts to copy sentences, but, while the size and arrangement of letters were good, the forms were not very accurate and there were some letter reversals. In Test A5 (Appendix A) she still made no attempt at any of the words and, when a sample of her reading ability was sought, she had no reader and was unable to suggest anything she could 'read'. By mid-November she had more writing in her classwork books, including further sentences written clearly for her by the teacher, but she could not read them. Her attempts at copying yielded a number of letter reversals in both the left–right and up–down sense, but copying was improving slowly.

In December Sara was still unable to recognise any word except *lorry* when it was shown to her on a page of the First Red Book. She did not seem interested in trying to read, or to expect ever to be able to do so. She reported that her mother could read, but that no one now read to her. This was a change from the previous year. Had her grandmother given up, and if so, why? Or had her previous report been fantasy? By February Sara could still read nothing. She was willing to talk about pictures in the Gay Way Red Book, but could recognise not a single word. She identified examples of letters quite spontaneously, pointing to several instances of *s*, *a*, *r* and *n*. She also suggested a *d* was a *b*. Since the letters she knew were in her own name, this was written as she watched, and she recognised it. She was interested in the whole conversation, but she said again that she did not want to learn to read.

By the third term of her second year her writing was seen to have improved, and she could confidently write her own name – indeed, under a misapprehension, when asked to write it in the top corner of a page, she was able to write it backwards with correct spelling (though with a reversed *a*). In a sentence copying task she wrote firm, clear letters, though she reversed some letters, and could not hold a steady line, or complete a copied sentence of more than about six words. When it came to a dictated sentence Sara was at sea, managing only a letter or two from her memory of some of the words. She could offer no spontaneous writing.

That she was just beginning to break into the Gay Way materials can be seen from the following report of a sampling in May.

Extract from the First Red Book (Gay Way)
The big red lorry went up the hill. The pots and pans went up the hill in the lorry.

Sara's reading (Age 6 years 6 months)
The red lorry went up the hill. The red lorry went up . . .

Sara now knew that the first sentence went with the accompanying picture, and apart from omitting *big* she recalled it. She had no idea of the second. She knew one or two words to the extent of being able to point them out, but she could not indicate *lorry* or *up*.

Part-way through this third term she was moved to another school. The arrangement by which she and her brother had been living with the grandmother came to an end when their parents felt they were able to offer a suitable home. How she would fare in another environment was difficult to estimate, for it had taken her the best part of two years to change from a shy, withdrawn, unsmiling little girl in school to one who had made friends, had learned her way about the school and among the people in it, was beginning to make recognisable progress in school-based skills, and was generally more responsive and cheerful. Her teachers were sorry to see her go and apprehensive about her future. Whatever other handicaps she laboured under, she seemed to face an uncertain future.

A report just over a year later from the headmaster of her new school was not very reassuring. Sara's parents had kept her with them and in the new school for a year, and then she had spent the summer with her grandmother before returning to her parents again. This entailed returning to her first school for July and September at the end of her third year and beginning of her fourth. It is hard to imagine a move more calculated to thoroughly unsettle a child.

In her new school she received supplementary teaching in a remedial small group for half a day each week. This gave her extra practice with phonics, writing and reading, and the personal attention and extra experience seemed to have helped her to improve her reading, though at 7 she was still well over a year behind the norm for her age. She was handicapped by her poor reading and writing when she tried other curriculum activities, but she also seemed to have difficulty concentrating and remembering even in oral activities. Furthermore, the many confusing aspects of her life seemed to have left her in a poor position to make friends with other children. Sara's slowness in learning to read was but one symptom of an almost overwhelming bewilderment and helplessness induced by her family circumstances.

FIONA

Fiona was a sturdy, pretty 5-year-old, of average height for the intake. She was at first rather shy of other children and adults, but she made no protest in spite of her obvious bewilderment with school life. Things happened around Fiona rather than to her. She gained confidence, however, during her first year in school, and in the second year had made friends. In her family she was the youngest of five girls; her father was a driver for a plumbing firm, and her mother was not working outside the home. Her health seemed good and her attendance at school was very good. At a medical examination, during her first year in school, defective hearing and faulty vision were both suspected but no defects were found on following this up. Her progress in school during the first two years was extremely slow, so that outside help was sought to advise on her education. It was decided that she should attend a special school, and a place was found for her during her third year. A talk with her mother when Fiona was 6 revealed some of the background to her learning problems. Her mother reported that she did not seem to want to talk about school or even to talk or do anything when she came home. When she asked her daughter about school she did not seem to remember what had happened. She had not taken to the teacher in her first year, but she was happier with the second. Her mother did not think Fiona could read any street or shop signs, but she could recognise the local bus numbers, and could write her name in a fashion. As will be seen later, her mother's account was a very fair description of Fiona's ability. As well as talking about her present state, however, she also spoke of her when she was a baby and toddler. The child had been slow to sit and walk. Her grandmother had been very helpful in bringing up the child, and had shown considerable patience in encouraging her with the various skills. It transpired that she had had experience of this with Fiona's mother when she was a baby; and the mother herself had had special schooling. None of Fiona's sisters, however, had needed special education, and her mother blamed her slow learning on a difficult birth. The impression gained from the talk with her mother suggested that she had had a careful upbringing, with much affection from both her mother and her grandmother. They had both tried to help her to learn to read, and had bought books for her. An older sister and her grandmother had read aloud to her from story-books; and her mother had told her stories, giving the impression that she was reading them, though in fact she was herself unable to read. There was a real concern to do her best for the child.

In spite of her shyness and bewilderment in her first months at school Fiona was quite willing to try tasks, especially drawing and copying. In these last her work was at first more like that of a 3–4-year-old, as was her speech and general understanding. In the various tasks intended to explore language abilities she showed even less ability to express a story or theme than Amanda, Sara, Matt and Michael, and even greater uncertainty and confusion in her ideas. This extended to her understanding of reading and writing, but although she seemed to have no idea of their significance she was willing to try to go along with the activities suggested by her teachers. In Tests A2 and A3 (Appendix A) she was unable to show any understanding of the terms *Number, letter, word* and *sentence*, though her responses included attempts to name a couple of letters phonically. Elements of some classroom learning could be detected.

When talking of reading, when she was 5, she mentioned that people did it by themselves, but she seemed to associate the word with ideas of drawing, of work and of holding pictures. She agreed to the idea that one could read newspapers and reported that her parents did so, but she tended either to evade answering questions about her parents or to fail to take her mind from her own line of thought. She volunteered the information that she had a book at home, bought for her by her father for Christmas. She could say nothing more about it, but she did say she would like to be able to read and that her mother would 'let her'. This sounded more like a reference to help, rather than permission, but one could not be sure.

In class she was making very little progress. She said she did not know any of the Breakthrough words on display, and she had no personal folder. She seemed unable to remember words and gave the impression of not really taking them in in the first place. She could draw pictures, and enjoyed drawing a snowman, and she had begun to copy patterns (as pre-writing experience) quite well.

When interviewed in March she was quite sure she could not read, but she was able to talk more freely about reading. She claimed to have a nursery-rhyme book at home, and she wanted to be able to read a book. She saw her parents as newspaper readers, not as readers of books, and she said her mother and a sister sometimes read to her at night in bed. (What this meant, given that her mother could not read, was obscure.) She said she tried to read to them, but not to her father. Again, reading must have meant something like talking about a book, story, or picture.

On both occasions of attempting the Breakthrough test, in April and June, she read nothing. She seemed to be totally at a loss to make anything of the words or sentences, but in July, while she still could not recognise any of the words, she was beginning to show some learning of the sounding of letters. She could sound *s* and *c* correctly and find other examples on a page of the Gay Way book. She could recognise *o* and *i* as 'round' and 'down' but could not find other examples. She said she could not remember any letters or words, and could not reliably point to examples of either in the test. She avoided a number of questions about the text but was willing to talk if she chose the topic. At one point she was asked if she could read anything of *I am Fiona*. She did not even recognise her name. She also showed no sign of visual analysis of words for she could see no similarities between *house* and *home*.

At the beginning of her second year she was willing to try to write her name, and she produced a string of ten letter-like symbols of which an initial *F* and a further two letters were recognisable. The remainder were indecipherable. In Test B2 (Appendix B) she successfully identified examples of big and little words and very slowly pointed to similar letters in initial positions in words, but she seemed not to grasp what was required in the other parts of the test. These required her to seek similarities between initial-, final- and middle-letter patterns, and to complete sentences presented orally. She seemed to have learned something of the distinction between words and letters and to be able to recognise a few letters, but to have made no further progress in the graphic analysis of words. The sentence completion task suggested that while she was capable of expressing meaning with reference to a given or completed state of affairs, she was not inclined to anticipate meanings. This would be a severe handicap in grasping novel situations and in seeking meaning from any context.

Fiona now had a sentence-maker for use in class – a new state of affairs for her. She had six words in it, to make the simple sentence *I love my mum and dad*. She also had a writing booklet in which she attempted to copy her name and various patterns modelled by the teacher. She had produced a very wobbly version of *Fiona* and her copying of strings of letters was very erratic. A string of *a*s included several reversals and unrecognisable squiggles. She was still not able to read any of the words in Test A5 (Appendix A), nor did she have a school reading book. She had no suggestion of anything she thought she might try to read.

By mid-November she had both number and writing books for her work in class. She was effectively practising the same skill in both, attempting to copy figures in one, and letter patterns and sentences in the other, though the discrimination of letters from numbers was also being achieved. Her copying, and even her tracing, of symbols was still very uncertain. The teacher had written the sentence-maker item *I love my mum and dad* for Fiona to copy, but she could not remember what it stood for when asked to read it or asked what it 'said'. With help she recited it, pointing to each word in turn, and repeating the whole. Ten minutes later she still remembered the sentence and could point to *dad*, *mum* and *and*. (She was not asked to indicate the other words.) The following week, however, she had again forgotten it all. During the second term of her second year when her approach to reading was explored again, she did not recognise any of the words in the First Red Book, but she did recognise (without prompting) the letter *s* which she sounded correctly. She said she knew *a* but pronounced it as *b*. She recognised her own name when it was written for her, but no other words – not even the *Class 4* and name of her teacher which appeared on her classroom door. She still indicated, however, that she thought she'd be able to read one day and that she would like to learn.

In May she wished to try a reading, with the following outcome.

Extract from the First Red Book (Gay Way)
The big red lorry went up the hill. The pots and pans went up the hill in the lorry.

Fiona's reading (Age 6 years 3 months)
The big lorry went up the hill. The big lorry went . . .

Fiona knew pretty well what the first sentence ought to be, and omitting *red* was her only mistake. She had no idea of the second. She seemed to have read the first more from a memory of associating it with the picture on the same page than from an ability to identify the words. Nevertheless, she was able to point successfully to *The* and *went* when asked, but not to *hill*.

In spite of her difficulties she still claimed to like reading, though she could give no reason or specify any aspect she liked or disliked. She mentioned Red and Yellow Gay Way books as those she liked best at school and home respectively. (This probably meant that she liked the pictures.) She also said it was hard for her to remember words, but pictures helped her to read. She could make no comment on the sounding and visual aspects of trying to read, or on the usefulness of reading to either children or adults. She said her mother tried to help her to read at home and that she tried to read to her mother. Moreover, she said she would like to read more in school. Thus in spite of such slight progress she was still cheerful and interested in trying to read.

Fiona's slow progress in school had caused her teachers much concern, and at this stage, after a thorough medical and psychological assessment, it was agreed with her parents that she should be transferred to a special school when a place became available. In the meantime it was decided to place her with the nursery class where her teacher could build on her existing skills, rather than keep her with a group who were outstripping her. She was moved to another school early in her third year, by which time her willing and cheerful attempt at the English Picture Vocabulary test had also yielded an assessment that suggested a need for special provision of some kind.

A report from the headteacher of her new school a year later was encouraging. With a further year of 'nursery-type' schooling and very simple pre-reading and early reading tasks Fiona had gained confidence and begun to read a little. Some very pleasant examples of Fiona's work with reading exercises such as word matching, following simple instructions, matching word to picture and matching word to phrase context were enclosed. Obviously Fiona was a generally slow learner but was by then able to respond to more detailed, step-by-step instruction that involved much repetition and practice.

SUMMARY

Compared with the children who began to learn to read during their first year at school, all five late beginners were unable to draw on much support at home, though for various reasons. They also showed a general slowness to learn in school, and had lower vocabulary scores. There did not seem to be any incapacitating language problems, but communication was hampered by Amanda's and Sara's emotional problems, Matt's shyness and relative immaturity, Michael's articulation handicap and Fiona's difficulty in comprehending. Moreover, the children were more inclined to look to their friends for help than to expect it or ask for it from adults. They seemed to take a long time to understand the teachers' and pupils' roles in school. On the other hand they were willing to do as they were told, so frequently they attempted tasks they did not comprehend.

They showed little understanding of the nature or purpose of reading when they came to school, and continued to find it elusive during their first year or two. Amanda's understanding, for example, seemed to develop as 'You remember what to say, and say it one word at a time', a strategy of dealing with an expectation that she try to read in a situation where she could scarcely match even one printed word with its spoken correlate. There was much evidence of willing copying of suggested sentences, but no corresponding ability to read them even a short while later. Understanding of the terms *letter*, *word* and *sentence* came slowly (though it is necessary to be able to recognise a word and sentence or two before such terms can become meaningful). This late understanding meant that many of the teachers' references to aspects of reading were lost.

Even in the face of a limited supply of words to be learned, these children made no progress, and thus failed to develop the awareness of orthography that soon emerged in those who began to learn.

Both Matt and Michael were hampered by problems with vision, but this was not the only cause of difficulty. Because they were obedient these children learned to name some letters phonically and later to try to sound words, but the lack of sufficient sight knowledge of a basic set of words and of letter patterning meant that neither meaning nor visual information could be looked to for cues, while the sounds they tried were not at all easily melded. Lack of strength on all three 'cue' fronts meant no progress. For a long time they faced words blankly, at best knowing that something might be said, but unable to guess what, unless a picture or some other background feature reminded them of what had been said before in that context. In Sara's case it was a long time before she realised that the correlate to a written word was a specific spoken one – not any one that might trip off the tongue!

Obviously these children needed help to bring them to the point of being able to do anything at all with written words, particularly to help them understand the communicative significance of reading and writing. They learned to perceive and copy patterns, and their talking improved, but their reading did not. The 'writing act' as distinct from the 'speech act' had to become meaningful.

Chapter 7

Literate Behaviour and Orthographic Knowledge

One of the aims defined in Chapter 1 was to explore children's understanding of the acts of reading and writing when they are beginning to learn to read. This might be termed understanding of literate behaviour. The second aim was to trace their developing knowledge of the spelling system, or orthographic knowledge. Before these are elaborated in the light of observations of the selected children, it is necessary to clear some theoretical ground which relates social background to the experience of learning to read.

Averages suggest that learning may be depressed by low socio-economic class and by deficiencies in schooling, but there is a danger that a record of success by quite a substantial proportion of pupils may be concealed. In the school in this study John and Wilma were typical of better-than-average and average readers, who altogether constituted about a third of the school intake; but home circumstances did seem to be detrimental to learning for many of the remainder. Such conditions were those typically found to occur more frequently in socially and economically disadvantaged areas, and to be associated with slow progress in the infant school. Chazan and Williams (1978) recently reported on the links between deprivation and education in a sample of urban primary schools, showing how children from deprived backgrounds learned far more slowly than those from settled working-class homes. It was found that although the latter began schooling with a slower move into reading than did middle-class children, they nevertheless responded well on the whole. Many children from deprived homes, on the other hand, were still engaged in pre-reading activities after a year in school and had not moved far through their reading schemes even after three years. At 7½ years about 40 per cent of such children had not reached a reading age of 6 years. The characteristic features of deprivation reported by Chazan and Williams were paternal employment in unskilled and semi-skilled jobs, a high degree of mobility, lack of home-ownership, overcrowding, a low level of parental education, low income leading to qualification for free school meals, and a high incidence of medical defects and disabilities. These features also characterised the neighbourhood in which John and his peers grew up, and, even where there were settled working-class families, a rising rate of unemployment was threatening family incomes and stability. Chazan and Williams mentioned a lack of concentration and poor language development as arising out of such background difficulties, and affecting learning to read; but the case studies reported in this book suggest a different interpretation of the relationship between deprivation and reading.

To take language development first, in the Chazan and Williams study poor language development was based on teachers' assessments of the pupils' state on starting school. During the first year in school, however, improvement was reported in articulation, spoken vocabulary and understanding of instructions and stories; yet little development in reading or number work was noted. A natural question to ask is how far was the initial assessment influenced by low expectations, or by difficulty in establishing communication with these children because of such factors as shyness and bewilderment, rather than inadequate language skills? Cases in this study suggest caution in assessing language development, especially at the point of entry to school, and show that socio-economic deprivation is neither a necessary nor a sufficient cause of poor language development in 5-year-olds.

But, allowing that delayed or deficient language development, when it does occur, may be thought to affect learning to read, it is important to ask whether this is so. It would seem from the examples of children who begin to read at about 3 years of age, from the elementary structures in early reading schemes, and from the possibility of using children's own suggestions as the raw material for reading, that linguistic competence in the narrow grammatical sense need not be particularly well developed for beginning reading. There is no good evidence in the research literature that handicap in the first stages of learning to read stems from this source. Furthermore, much the same argument applies in the case of vocabulary, with the qualification that there may be words in early reading schemes that are unknown to the child. In such instances explanation is called for, or some adjustment might be made to the scheme. Vocabulary mismatch need not be a handicap. It may be true that relatively underdeveloped syntax and vocabulary prove an increasing handicap as further reading is attempted, but, equally, reading may itself prove to be a source of further language development. Ability to use language in various ways may also bear on learning to read, but it is difficult to see that a child who can talk with a teacher about classroom activities, can follow instructions of various kinds, can attempt explanations and can ask questions, is not in a position to benefit from help with learning to read. The only questions that were raised from this study were whether children were handicapped by inability to give a coherent account, vagueness or confusion in their understanding, or unwillingness to accept 'invented' or fantasy statements as legitimate in the context where truth is expected; but these bore as much on questions of cognition and understanding as they did on language.

A further possibility is that manner of speaking may interfere with reading. Now it may be the case that speech defects do so, either directly or by hampering communication, but dialect is another matter. Since the half of the children in this study who did make progress showed the same dialect features as those who did not (and John was representative of a fair number of children with a strong dialect who became able readers), it can scarcely be claimed that it necessarily has a retarding effect. Indeed, there were interesting indications that the children had no difficulty understanding either text or teachers' spoken English, and they even adapted their own speech towards such models when reading aloud or telling stories. Altogether these considerations lead to a sharing of Stubbs's (1980) view that poor language development is unlikely to be a major cause of failure in the first stages of learning to read.

Chazan and Williams also mentioned poor concentration in children from deprived areas, but this may have been related to a lack of understanding of what was required. When Sara, Amanda, Fiona, Matt, or Michael were playing games that they had invented, or were occupied with tasks they understood, they seemed able to sustain attention well enough. It was only when things became incomprehensible that attention wavered and was turned elsewhere. Apparent lack of attention may be due to the bewilderment felt by many youngsters on entering school. The full impact of school can only be gauged through the kind of informal conversation with the children that the design of this study made possible, for somehow one must get near to participating in the child's life in school in order to understand it. What children in this study conveyed through their actions, questions and comments was that they were trying to work out what schooling was about. Home was familiar; daily lives made sense in terms of what they and members of the family and friends usually did in the course of the day; and for the most part, children knew what was expected of them, and what they might do. School made no such sense, and children were trying to find some aspect that was personally meaningful and around which they could operate.

Some had more immediate success than others. It is quite likely that school activities seem more sensible to children who have crayons, paints, plasticine, paper, books, bricks, marbles, jigsaws, 'dressing-up' clothes and other such playthings at home than they do to children who have not, especially if they are accustomed to adults taking an interest in their play, sharing activities with them, and telling or reading them stories. The gulf between home and school for some of the children from disadvantaged backgrounds was large. According to the mothers interviewed, money for playthings was not always available; even where it was, the toys did not reflect school-based activities very much, and very few books or comics were bought. For the most part parents did not lack affection for their children or interest in their welfare, but they had little understanding of schools and schooling and of the different life-styles that education might make attainable. This is not to say that school was not appreciated, for gratitude was expressed by some for the various social services performed by and through it. Support and advice for parents in times of need, the child-minding function of school and medical attention for the children were but three of these services. It was as though the time and energy of teachers were being incorporated into the parental responsibilities of the neighbourhood, but there was little awareness or thought among parents of educational responsibility. Only if their children pressed them did parents try to help. Even reading to the children was not linked with schooling but was seen as a part of the life of the family, parents telling stories which had once been told to them in their own childhood, and associated with the bed-time ritual of the post-toddler years. School was a place apart and literacy was little understood.

This gulf was reflected in the children's comments about many activities, including reading. Mostly they had some idea of newspapers and of a limited selection of books, but some children, such as Michael and Sara, really did not know at all what reading might mean. Moreover, their attention had not been drawn to writing in their everyday environment. They did not seem to know about reading bus numbers and destinations, advertisements, shop names and the many other written signs and indicators. Imagine the bewilderment of such children when expected to use labelling in the classroom, to recognise a written word or sentence and to manipulate word cards to form sentences! The whole set of school pre-reading behaviours was incomprehensible, and certainly not easily talked about. Teachers of such children could be forgiven if they mistakenly assessed language skills as poor. Yet, when activities did make sense, whether early, as in John's case, or late, as in Matt's, then children could talk about them, learn about them and so make progress. For many of the children such sense had to be established *within school*, and this necessarily took time.

Downing (1979) has considered those aspects of children's understanding of reading and of the terminology of reading instruction that have featured in research literature such as that of Reid (1966), Downing (1970), Clay (1972) and Francis (1973), and has subsumed them in his general concept of cognitive clarity. This emphasis on the cognitive tasks in learning to read is important, for not only does it draw attention to matters that require the attention of teachers when considering how best to work with their pupils, but it also suggests that confusions and misapprehensions of various kinds may be stumbling blocks for individuals. The studies in this book lend support to the generally accepted point that a lack of clarity in understanding may be associated either with deprivation of experience of literacy in the home, or with a more pervasive cognitive vagueness which is reflected generally in a child's conversation and performance in tasks in school. They also illustrate the specific misunderstandings and lack of insight that may attend any pupil's learning. In all cases strategies of learning and patterns of development were affected.

The major problems of understanding the nature of reading and of learning to read which faced at least five of the ten children were based in the combination of finding the task in school somewhat incomprehensible and of having no particularly relevant prior or background experience to draw on. What did they do to cope with the situation? Their first strategy was to watch, listen and try to do what they were told. They looked to the teacher for overall guidance about where they were to go and what they were to do. Thus they were able to attempt tasks such as drawing, copying, listening to stories and repeating the teacher's words, at least at the level of performing the required kind of action. But, unlike Wilma and John, they neither understood what reading or writing might be for themselves, nor saw any link between these pre-reading activities and adults' reading of newspapers, comics, or books. Indeed, they depended to some extent on children who did grasp the tasks to provide a model of what the teacher wanted. Somehow this kind of dependence, combined with a feeling that children's play was not the kind of thing they expected adults to be interested in, prompted them to seek help from their peers rather than from the teacher, unless the latter was directly and personally involved in what they were doing.

These strategies had some, albeit limited, pay-off. All the children, however poor their skill, became better able to copy script, all gained some idea of the use of labelling, all became better able to understand and engage in conversation about stories and classroom activities, all gained in confidence about actually managing life in the classroom, but there was no pay-off in terms of meaningful new learning about reading. They could not ask because they did not know what eluded them; and although some of their peers began to read and enjoy reading, they either had no expectation that this might happen to them or they expected it to 'happen' some time in the future. Their lack of understanding inclined them towards learning by rote. They began by making some headway with sight methods of word learning, whether this was of isolated words or of sentences. Such rote strategies may in fact be appropriate when meeting the first words, but unless learning becomes in some sense meaningful, there comes a point where passive memorising fails. The Breakthrough reading scheme is intended to support meaningful learning, for children meet new words in sentences which have some relevance to their own experience. But it became obvious that for some children active sentence construction was a non-starter, for while they copied and repeated sentences the teacher or other children provided, they had no idea of doing this themselves. It was as though they had no access to their knowledge of spoken language for this kind of exercise. While John and others who were learning to read in their first year in school could think about words and statements in their speech, and for them speaking a word that was being looked at evoked memories of using that word in speech, for children like Amanda, Dave, Michael, Sara and Matt no such thought or links seemed to be made until much later. Their early attempts to remember 'sight' words and sentences were neither enthusiastic nor effective. At first each new word failed to find a link in the mesh of understanding and so fell right through the sieve.

What is central to understanding literate behaviour is comprehension of the nature of the acts of reading and writing – that they function as acts of communication in a similar way to talking and listening. Linguistic philosophers have analysed the speech act in a way that is particularly helpful here. The speaker is seen as intending by his utterance to influence a hearer to believe or do what he says, and the effectiveness of the act depends on the hearer's recognition of that intention. If this is applied to literate behaviour then the writer must be seen as intending to influence the reader similarly, and the reader must recognise this intention. The question that arises is how far children have grasped this when required to learn to read. Soderbergh's (1971) study showed how realisation came to a 3-year-old through the process of learning to read and handle words meaningfully in the context of communicating with and about them. It is easy for the literate adult to forget that the act of writing does not come to the child in the same way as does the speech act. Spoken language develops through use, necessity even, as soon as the child is able to articulate with intended meaning. Writing cannot be managed so early in life and, being a second verbal signalling system, does not carry the same strong functional need. It is learned with an awareness of action which is not present in the very small child's talking and only gradually overtakes his speaking.

Children who have not learned to reflect on speech may need the whole idea of communicative function to be made explicit before they really grasp what literacy is all about and gain any real urge to learn to read and write, and any useful understanding of what teachers are trying to do. Pre-reading experiences should include not only drawing and copying and playing with both written and spoken words, but also play at sending genuine messages by mouth, by picture and by writing, together with discussion about how messages 'work'. It may also be necessary to help children understand differences between invention and truth in authorship. While they may distinguish between listening to stories and talking in everyday life, and be prepared to read stories, however improbable, they may be disturbed by being required to invent sentences or stories themselves, confusing such invention with fabrication. Soderbergh's child, as described in Chapter 1, made this difficulty clear; but a bewildered child trying to please a relatively strange adult in school may not do so, but may simply, and unhappily, withdraw or be too worried to learn. In this study some of the children were worried by being asked to suppose various states of affairs in some of the language tasks. They were only prepared to deal with what they knew to be the case. Even those who are not worried, like John, may see much sentence construction, even if true, as meaningless, because it is neither a proper story nor intended as an everyday act of communication. Many observations in this study suggested that children deprived of literary experience at home might benefit considerably from a thoroughgoing introduction to understanding of authorship and readership, and that this could be more important than devising reading schemes supposedly appealing to relevance rather than fantasy.

The second major focus of this study was the way children gained knowledge of the spelling system of written language. Although English traditional orthography has frequently been criticised for its lack of simple letter–sound correspondence, and so is said to be an obstacle in learning to read, linguists in recent years have pointed out various systematic relations between spelling patterns and the organisation of words around common roots. In such a context apparently functionless letters are shown to have their uses in helping to mark and distinguish groups, as are letters which are sounded in some contexts but not others, for in drawing attention to the root of a word they facilitate interpretation. The historical development of orthography makes much linguistic sense, but it is a story of adult literacy and technological change. Children of various ages and interests have always had a 'look-in', but only recently has it been thought necessary to try to see that all children learn to read at a relatively early age, and teaching methods have not always taken seriously enough the nature of orthography and what children can do with it.

Spelling has generally been regarded as a writing skill, and of no major interest until children can read and write a little. Research interest in it is now reviving after a period of quiescence, but any consideration of the nature of orthography points to the fact that both reading and writing are implicated. In this study a distinction has been made between the ability to spell, in the sense of performing the correct sequencing of letters in writing or in oral spelling of a word, and knowledge of orthography or the underlying system of spelling. Children might be able to recognise aspects of system through patterns before they can write more than a few words correctly and before they can pronounce some of the words they see; and such knowledge would begin to grow from their very earliest acquaintance with script, provided they see enough of it. This would be as true of any other alphabet-based orthography as of the traditional form used in this study. The initial teaching alphabet, for example, also shows systematic relations between letters in words. Its advantage over traditional orthography is claimed to be in the way it encodes more simply some of the more complex patterns of spelling. Knowledge of spelling patterning has here been termed orthographic competence, and an attempt has been made to trace signs of its development by exploring various ways children used cues in text to help them remember words and to try to read new ones. This could only be done with those children who began to make some progress, so little of value was observed in the case studies reported in Chapter 6. Nevertheless, what there was, was not inconsistent with the following account.

From the first, John, Wilma, Mary and Sean were able to make use of sufficient cues to help them recognise some of the words they had seen before, and to distinguish one from another. Although they did not learn all the alphabet, they quickly learned some useful letters, named then 'phonically', and could identify them in print. By the beginning of their second year their responses to Test B2 (Appendix B) showed that they could see similarities and differences between words on the basis of pairs or other patterns of letters. They were able to use visual cues when trying to recognise words, and were in a position to learn something of English spelling. Of the four, Wilma and John showed this kind of visual pattern perception over whole words, though Mary and Sean seemed to find some difficulty attending to complex information towards the ends of words. For all four children errors in reading were frequently visually similar to the word in the text. It was as though a decision had to be made between several similar items in memory, a 'near miss' sometimes being the result.

But using visual cues was not their only strategy. To varying extents they used context cues. Quite early they expected words to fit the limited sentence-frames they had encountered. Later, like other children in their class who could try to read a sentence or two, they could read words in familiar contexts better then in word lists (Francis, 1977). This was apparent in the first Breakthrough test and during their attempts to read from the Gay Way book in their first year. Misreadings sometimes showed the influence of the sense of the text rather than visual similarity to the word concerned, but often the errors suggested recourse to both kinds of cue. At first context cues gave misreadings that were grammatically appropriate and sensible, though in relation to that part of a sentence already read rather than to the whole sentence. An error, however, frequently 'threw' the rest of the sentence. In the early stages, too, what was familiar was very limited, and misreadings did not venture outside this restricted pool. For children who did not start with John's and Wilma's advantages an early type of cue was an accompanying picture. Here the child thought that the object of the exercise was to say something about what was illustrated, whether or not it bore any resemblance to the text sentence. A later-used cue was position or page in the book, where reading was seen as saying something following what was remembered as going before. This resulted in 'reading' a sentence which followed the remembered one but was not the one at hand. The quicker readers had not seemed to use such cues, either because they were less tied to a rather passive association learning, or because they had sufficient insight into reading to know they had to attend more precisely to the particular text they were trying to read. Once the later readers did attend more closely to the text, their misreadings showed both graphic and context suitability.

But to return to the quicker readers: their performances had much in common, but with interesting individual variations. What seemed strange during the first year was the relative lack of use of phonic cues in trying to read, in spite of readiness to respond appropriately in teaching situations. The children used phonics to *name* letters rather than to sound and blend. Not until the summer of his first year, when he was already reading beyond the Gay Way Red Book level, did John spontaneously, or in response to suggestion, try to sound a word. When he was trying to recall what he had read previously he showed no sign of needing to use other than visual and context cues, and he later slipped smoothly into successfully attempting new words, for the most part without explicit sounding.

Wilma, on the other hand, was less willing to guess and, as shown in her misreadings, was highly dependent on visual cues in the early stages. She took the meaning of what she could recognise but did not use it to anticipate what followed. Like John, however, she did not try phonic cues until the first summer; but, unlike him, she was pleased to find this new kind of cue, though at about the same time she was also reading with some anticipation of meaning. Mary, too, did not begin to seek phonic cues until the first summer term, but she had by then gained a more limited hold over visual cues than had John and Wilma, and she was not in a good position to use either derived or anticipated meaning. Sean, on the other hand, was the first of the sample explicitly to seek to use phonic cues. Even before Easter in his first year, when he could scarcely recall any of the words he had come across, he mentioned sounding as a way of trying to read a word. Moreover, he spontaneously tried sounding words during the summer term, and at the same time showed improved word recognition without explicit sounding. But his reading was much less fluent and much more confined to a limited pool of words than was the case for the other three children.

In the second and third years John had little recourse to any explicit phonic cues. It was during the early months of his second year, when his horizons broadened to a wider range of reading, that he sometimes used sounding to help himself. He disliked doing so because it slowed him down, but he needed the extra cues when faced with a new word and insufficient visual and context cues to determine a meaningful solution. Then he did not necessarily sound the whole word, but only enough of it to enable a limited range of possible words to spring to mind from which he could select the context-appropriate candidate. This seemed to be the way newly seen words gained mental storage space and, later, recognition via the visual memory route. With this strategy, what could be seen could be converted to what could be said in order to discover its meaning, not simply to read it aloud. This was a critical step, and the only point at which John made any obvious use of explicit sounding. Very soon his reading became so fluent that only experimental techniques could have been used to probe his use of cues, but he was probably using context, visual and subvocal cues in a complex, well-integrated way. It was clear that at no time in his learning had he shown evidence of having to attend explicitly or consciously to the full visual or phonic information available from the written or spoken word. This gives food for thought.

Wilma, however, did try to attend to all the letters in words. This did not prevent her from gaining the meaning of what she read, but it slowed her down, and it inclined her to try to conquer new words more by complete sounding than by sounding just enough to cue the correct version from sense. Not until well into her third year did she move more easily into anticipatory reading which required less reliance on complete word information. It was interesting that her greater use of explicit sounding did not appear to accelerate her move into wider reading, but rather to help fill a gap by giving her partial access until she was ready to seek, rather than to accept, meaning. Although Mary made less progress than Wilma in her first year, she attempted sounding during her second, showing some successful use. But this was intermittent. She did not use it readily as a way of helping herself when visual and context cues failed, so it was in no way a compensatory strategy. Similarly, Sean struggled slowly through his second and third years, able to analyse and synthesise the sounding of regular words, but unable to use the strategy to compensate for his problems with the visual grasp of orthography. In the case of the slow readers, Dave and Matt were able to try to use phonic cues towards the end of their second year, but they were unable to do so easily and had made very little progress with visual recognition and with the use of context cues. For Michael, Amanda, Sara and Fiona, only very preliminary moves to use cues of various kinds were being made, and neither the breakdown of speech into sounds nor that of written words into letters was at all well advanced, even in the third year.

Overall, then, there was much less evidence of recourse to sounding strategies than to others, in spite of the basing of initial words on spoken sentences and an early introduction to the idea of using sound cues. It was as though the children learned something of an explicit technique that for the most part they did not need to, or could not, use in actual reading. There was, on the other hand, plenty of evidence of early systematic learning of the spelling system. These observations lead to consideration of the nature and significance of this learning and its importance in forging links between spoken and written language. What has to be accounted for is how some children can learn to read fluently without using much, if any, explicit phonics, and why others, who can use phonics to some extent, are reluctant to do so until they show a fair use of visual and contextual cues, that is, until they show some orthographic competence and some ability to construct meaning from text.

It seems possible that if a sufficient grounding in visual word recognition is established a grasp of orthography can follow, such that links can be made with spoken language which enable further reading without an explicit phonic approach. In the case of the Soderbergh child, described in Chapter 1, this clearly happened; and there are also other research reports which show the growth of a knowledge of English spelling under various kinds of 'Look and Say', non-phonic, teaching (MacKinnon, 1959; Barr, 1974). Consideration of misreadings, known more recently as mis-cue analysis, typically shows the way errors are influenced by context and by graphic similarity between the suggested and the target word. (Reading when phonic methods are employed also shows these kinds of mis-cue, but additionally there are errors of partial and nonsense pronunciation, such as those shown by the slower learners in this study when trying to sound words.) The key to understanding how reading may progress without explicit phonics must lie in the way developing orthographic competence is combined with what is linguistically meaningful for the child. A detailed consideration of this development is required, two concepts being involved – visual information processing and linguistic meaningfulness.

A standard source of information on visual perception and processing relating to reading is Gibson and Levin (1975). The evidence from the present study goes further in suggesting a developmental trend from a recognition of the spaced integrity of words in text, and of letters in words, to some knowledge of letter patterning in English words. Misreadings at first tended to be guesses from words already seen and remembered as written words. A child who has only met one written word can do nothing but recognise it or fail to do so, but when he has seen more than one, he has a selection to choose from and, if he detects no clue, can only guess. There was much evidence of such guessing by children in this study, but later misreadings began to show selection in line with graphic similarity to the desired word. At first it was perhaps only one letter in common, but as the children encountered words again and again they began both to be more accurate in recognition and to give misreadings which had two or more letters in common, often also sharing some position or order feature. They also began to show awareness of pattern and similarity. Further experience enabled familiar short words to be seen embedded in longer ones. Finally, children who were making progress with reading were able to distinguish permitted and non-permitted English spellings in nonsense words.

It might be claimed that this growth of orthographic knowledge depended on letter and pattern identification derived from explicit phonics teaching, but although benefit seemed to accrue from the naming of letters which was incidental to phonics, much of the pattern recognition appeared when the children were as yet unable to sound individual letters in order to blend sounds into words, and had received no teaching about sounding digraphs. Lest it be thought the evidence from the children in this study is slight, the reader is also referred to the findings of a wider sampling of reading by a much larger number of children from different schools. Misreadings showing graphic similarity, which could be taken as evidence of developing orthographic knowledge, were very common in the early stages of reading whether or not any phonics teaching had been attempted (Francis, 1977).

More developed knowledge of orthography is referred to by Henderson and Chard (1980), who reviewed research into the reading skills of children of 7 years and older. Various experimental tasks such as recognition under rapid decision conditions, searching for target letters and comparisons between items show that children are more successful with words than with pseudo-words and random-letter sequences, in that order. Although success with pseudo-words might be due to pronounceability, it is not the case that all true words are obviously pronounceable. Orthographic organisation seemed to be involved, but, because the effect was also found with mixed upper- and lower-case lettering, this was thought to imply systematic knowledge rather than superficial perceptual association. Henderson and Chard proposed some kind of letter-within-word coding, affected by orthographic regularity. Tacit, and even partial, knowledge might be sufficient to aid reading; but explicit and more determinate knowledge might be needed for accurate spelling. (It will be argued below that it might also be necessary for reading for some children or for some situations.) This is precisely the conclusion towards which this book tends with its developmental tracing of possible tacit and partial knowledge of orthography and of the use of sounding in reading.

The distinction between tacit and explicit knowledge relates to the second concept mentioned above – linguistically meaningful. This is a complex term which should be carefully unpacked. It can have at least three levels of application in relation to the child's experience of verbal expression. The basic level is that of the direct understanding of speech in everyday use. Initial reading makes comparatively little demand on this level, the knowledge of an average 3-year-old giving plenty to work on, but while it is available for linking with visual representations, it is not a sufficient condition for learning to read. A second level is that of understanding that verbal expressions can themselves be talked about. This implies not only a use of language, but also an awareness of it as a particular kind of phenomenon. Understanding mother saying something captures meaning at the first level. Being able to say that mother said something suggests linguistic meaning at the second level. This further level is entailed in much of the verbal play that children experience in their early years and it promotes the idea that verbal expression can be represented. The Soderbergh child's discussion of the problems of representing different parts of speech illustrates this and shows how the idea enables links with visual representation to be made. This level of linguistic meaningfulness, awareness of verbal expression as an object of attention, appeared to elude the slower learners in this study and seems to be a further necessary condition for learning to read.

The third level is awareness of the linguistic structuring of oral and written expressions. Certain aspects of knowledge of such structuring seem to be necessary to link written with spoken language, and they rest on either tacit or explicit recognition that verbal expressions can be talked about and that they can be subjected to processes of analysis and synthesis. Utterances can be broken down into words, and words can be combined to form utterances. Written sentences can represent utterances, and can be treated similarly; moreover, spoken words can be analysed into sound patterns, and visual forms into letter patterns, in ways such that at least some correspondences can be identified. Phonics teaching makes such analysis and synthesis of words explicit and gives various correspondence rules in order to aid initial reading. Whether such explicit analysis is a necessary condition for learning, whether it is something children become able to do incidentally in the course of learning, and whether it is more helpful for some children than others, or at some stages of learning than at others, are empirical questions awaiting answers. If it is not a necessary condition then it would be the case that children can normally learn through unconscious linking of processes of visual pattern analysis (orthographic knowledge), of which they are unaware, with processes of phonetic pattern analysis of which they are equally unaware. Since pronunciation of words in association with their visual form, and aided by their use in contexts which are understood in speech, seems to enable at least some children to learn to read, then explicit phonics seems not to be a necessary condition. Such a conclusion is entirely in harmony with what is known of spoken language acquisition.

Children learn to operate complex patterns and regularities without any conscious discrimination or analogy. Such unconscious processes for treating complex information of all kinds seem to be basic to the human condition.

But children are not equally skilled at the complex visual processing that underlies orthographic competence, and it does not necessarily follow that explicit phonics should be excluded from teaching reading. It becomes important to ask when and how awareness of detail of linguistic form might be useful. Research literature is not too helpful here, for although it is recognised that word meaning can be tapped through either sight or sound (Coltheart, 1978; Bryant and Bradley, 1980), discussion of the use of the two routes rests mostly on experiment and observation with children who can already read. Moreover, it rarely rests on true reading as distinct from the recognition or reading of single words. From such work as has been reported it generally seems to be thought that visual memory can serve to evoke meaning, but that reading new words requires some ability to link seen words with sound-analysed words, and so understand them through spoken language.

There are several difficulties if this view is applied to learning to read. It fails to take into account children's use of context cues of various kinds, which enable them to reduce uncertainty when memory fails or when a word is new. Secondly, it ignores the considerable extent to which children gain generalisable orthographic knowledge during the establishment of the visual route. Thirdly, it does not explain how children become aware of phonological units (phonemes) to associate with letters, when what they hear is phonetic. Phonology, after all, is an abstract description of the phonic regularities in speech as it relates to the meaning of words within utterances. Rather than using explicit knowledge of phonemic descriptions to identify letter patterns in new words, so gaining their meaning through sounding them, it is just as likely, if not more so, that children identify letters and letter patterns that evoke sounds associated with similar-looking words and so cue spoken words which fit the context. Such phonetic cueing would be most likely to succeed at first with single letters or digraphs which had been seen fairly frequently in known words and whose associations with phonetic sound could be represented as relatively invariant one-to-one phoneme–grapheme correspondences. Any such associations could be made entirely unconsciously, but letters in written words and the sounds of spoken words could also be talked about if the child noticed them or was encouraged to notice them, that is, if the third level of linguistic awareness were fostered. It would be difficult to tell, however, if explicit encouragement either to break spoken words into sounds or to sound the letters of seen words would necessarily add anything of value to emerging reading skill, and it would almost certainly be the case that phonically graded reading materials would lend themselves quite usefully to a visual approach supplemented by phonetic cues, which is how efficient learners may use them.

If, on the other hand, the development of orthographic knowledge were to be hampered through relatively poor visual memory or lack of sufficient experience of associating seen words with their meanings, then phonics teaching might be valuable to strengthen learning and enable meaning to be captured by overt sounding of much, if not all, of a word. It is worth noting in this context that it has been claimed that the children who seem to gain most from phonic approaches tend to come from less advantaged backgrounds. They may well lack experience of attending to seen words, and therefore be in much the same position at first as children whose visual information processing is not strong. They will be able to see individual letters in words, and to recognise them in different contexts, but not be able to see patterns, even frequent patterns, at all readily. They will find it hard to discriminate visually between words, and so to anchor what is seen in its spoken correlates. Thus the unconscious linking of orthographic coding with phonetic, which characterises the fluent early reader, cannot be achieved. For such children it is almost impossible to move from early 'Look and Say' learning, and even this takes only a precarious hold. It is possible that more help with reading at home might assist them (and so might a deliberate extension of their experience with words in school, even if they have difficulty recalling them), for they often miss the experience of seeing and trying to read print that more advantaged children enjoy, and there is evidence that those who do have this experience are better readers (Francis, 1975; Hewison and Tizard, 1980).

For some children, then, orthographic competence might be improved by wider exposure to signs and text. One of the risks of the Breakthrough approach was that of restricting children to their own limited sentence-maker vocabulary. Yet, together with others whose difficulties do not lie in lack of experience of text but in grasp of complex visual pattern, they may require a supplementary approach through phonics. Clay (1969) took the view that concentration on one type of cue might be better for the less able than asking them to spread their energies over three types, as the more able do, and that in some cases concentration on phonics would be indicated. There are, however, differing views as to how phonics should be taught, and it may be that the concept of orthographic competence introduced in this book is helpful in assessing them, and in particular in weighing up the usefulness of teaching children to attach sounding to written words against that of teaching them to analyse the sound structure of spoken words before seeing them in print. Pidgeon (1976) favours the latter as the more logical approach, within an overall analysis of the child's development of language skills; but only in cases of severe deprivation of experience of literacy is it likely to happen that such a sequence can be strictly adhered to.

Nevertheless, whether or not they see words in print, children like Sean and Dave, whose development of orthographic competence was seriously in question, might benefit from such an approach. Since they cannot readily use overall sentence and word patterns as cues, then such children are forced to tackle reading word by word and letter by letter. To know how the constituent sounds of words might be represented by single letters, digraphs, or further multiple-letter groups could be necessary armoury for tackling text. To try to analyse written words into letter units to yield sounds to be blended into words would be extraordinarily difficult, for these children would have no tendency to identify relevant multiple-letter groups or context regularities. They would appreciate nothing of such pattern until considerable practice in relating sound-analysed spoken words to seen words had given them the necessary experience. What is known of children's ability to sound-analyse spoken words suggests that learning to read in this way is likely to be delayed compared with learning based on the direct acquisition of some knowledge of the spelling system. But even for those children who can acquire this knowledge directly, phonics can be usefully taught via letter pattern to sound correspondences, though training in blending may be unnecessary if partial sounding can be used to top up cues from sight and meaning. It seems likely from these considerations that instruction in phonics is best planned in relation to what is known of the child's complex visual pattern perception abilities and the development of what has here been termed his orthographic competence.

It is clear that much unconscious information processing, of both spoken and written material, accompanies learning to read; but conscious analysis of both at the third level of linguistic awareness is characteristic at some point of most children's learning. The extent to which it is done varies among children and may be much more evident in one mode than in the other. Indeed, marked imbalance may be shown in children who can read better than they can spell, and vice versa (Bryant and Bradley, 1980). Moreover, the growth of such awareness in one seems to trigger or facilitate that in the other.

For many children, the ability to analyse and compare seen words seems to precede that with spoken words (Francis, 1973, 1975), but this may simply reflect the easier experience of comparing items presented concurrently and continuously (words on paper) rather than those presented sequentially and intermittently (heard words). What is made conscious, however, is not a knowledge of structuring such as is captured in linguists' theories of syntax and phonology, but simply the knowledge that both written and spoken language do have recognisable regularities, and can usefully be taken apart and put together again the better to convey and grasp intended meanings. This is a further understanding of literate behaviour. The underlying coding remains obscure, as indeed it still does to a large extent for linguists and for those interested in brain and mental processes, but the outcome of unconscious information processing in relation to text is the development of some knowledge of system in spelling, even with such a complex orthography as that of English. This knowledge guides performance in both reading and writing, not in the sense that it guarantees accuracy, but in the sense that it helps the child to make appropriate decisions and provides the framework for the growth of greater precision in performance.

Some readers may have recognised, in the terms literate behaviour and orthographic competence, analogies with the notions of communicative and syntactic competence used in descriptions of natural language acquisition. Such similarity is intended, for, although learning to talk and learning to read are early achievements, they are both complex cognitive and social skills, while the spoken and written forms of language are both 'rule-governed' modes of expression. This exploration of the terms in relation to children's learning may have helped to clarify the process, pinpoint the problems and point towards strategies of teaching.

The basic conclusions of this book are twofold. First, it is worth attending to children's understanding of literate behaviour both before and during the school years, this being a much more complex matter than reading to them. Secondly, it is worth exposing children to a sufficient set of written words (carrying communicative meaning for them) for their natural visual processing skills to begin to develop orthographic knowledge and so facilitate the development of reading, however it might be taught. The discussion leading to these conclusions has raised empirical questions which can only be tackled by further research, for although the phenomenon of orthographic competence can be deduced from existing research literature, study of its nature, origin and development is virtually unexplored territory.

Appendix A: Tests Used in the First Year of Observation (children aged 5 years)

TEST A I

Ask each child to copy the array below on to a sheet of A4 paper.

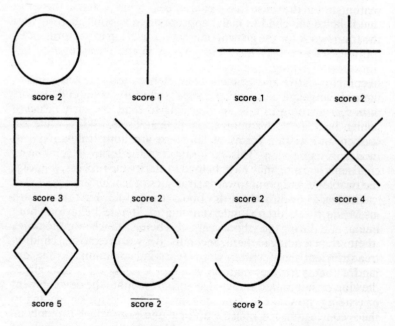

(Actual dimensions: 1" width for each figure.)

TEST A2: DISCRIMINATION OF LETTERS AND NUMBERS

(1) Present the card illustrated below (actual dimensions 5″ × 3″).

a	c
4	8

Pointing to each item in turn ask: Is this a number? Can you read it, or tell me what it is?

(2) Present the card illustrated below (actual dimensions 5″ × 3″).

m	2
3	t

Pointing to each item in turn ask: Is this a letter? Can you read it, or tell me what it is?

TEST A3: DISCRIMINATION OF TERMS 'LETTER', 'WORD' AND 'SENT-ENCE'

(1) Ask: Can you tell me a letter? And another?
Repeat for *word* and *sentence*.

(2) Spread the nine cards shown below (actual dimensions 5″ × 3″) before the child.
Ask: Can you show me a letter? And another letter?
Reapeat for *word* and *sentence*.
(If the child indicates a letter within a word, or a word within a sentence, rephrase the question to indicate a card with a letter/word on it, or a letter/word by itself.)

(3) Pointing to each of the cards in turn, ask the child to read it.

Array of cards for Test A3:

He is a boy	w	cat
o	girl	It is a dog
cup	I like my house	m

TEST A4: READING QUESTIONNAIRE

In a relaxed setting ask the child the following questions, wording them as seems best for each child:

(1) (*a*) Can you read yet?
  (*b*) Why are you learning to read?
  (*c*) Have you any books at home to read or look at? What is in them? Have you any books at school to read or look at? What is in them?
  (*d*) What do you think you will read when you are bigger?
  (*e*) What does Daddy read? What does Mummy read? Do they read quietly by themselves?
  (*f*) Does anybody at home read out loud to you? Who? When? (Try to gauge frequency – not very often, quite often, nearly every day.)
  (*g*) Do you try to read out loud to anybody? Who? What? When?
  (*h*) Can you write your name for me? Can you write anything else? Tell me about what you have written.

(2) (*a*) Show me your classroom reading book, the one your teacher is helping you to make. Can you read it to me?

(*b*) (Show the child the First Gay Way Red Book.) Is this a hard book to read? Have you tried to read it to the teacher? Is it harder than your first book? What is hard about it?

(*c*) (Show the first page, or ask the child to show the page he has reached, as appropriate.) Can you read this for me?

(*d*) How do you know what it says?

(*e*) What do you do if you don't know and want to find out?

(*f*) Do the pictures help?

(*g*) If you can read a bit, and then come to a word you don't know, what can you do? What else can you do?

(*h*) Show me a hard word. What is hard about it? Is there anything else that makes it hard?

(*i*) What are these spaces for? (between words).

(*j*) Are all these words? (indicating all print on page).
(If the answer is negative) Which aren't words? What are they?

(3) Can you write something from your own reading book? Show me. How do you know what to put?

(4) (*a*) Show me your sentence-maker. What can you do with it?

(*b*) Can you make a sentence for me?

(*c*) Can you read the sentence?

(*d*) Can you read this? (Construct a sentence, e.g. *I am at school*.)
Is this a sentence? (Same words in a different sentence order, e.g. *am I at school*.) Can you read it?
And is this a sentence? (Same words in nonsense order, e.g. *at am school I*.) Can you read it?

(*e*) (Repeat above, if useful, with another example such as *Ben is a dog*.)

(*f*) Are these words like (nearly the same as, etc.) each other?
(i) Show *play* and *went* as a pair for comparison, then *down* and *have*.
(ii) Show *house* and *home* for comparison, then *hill* and *mill*.
How are they the same/different?

TEST A5: THE BREAKTHROUGH READING TEST

(1) Ask the child to read the following, pointing to each word in turn. (Words arranged on a card as below but in Breakthrough script.)

boy	the	house
television	a	dog
like	home	can
cat	girl	good
big	at	baby
I	little	he
birthday	in	we
is	it	am
school	on	my
are	bed	see

(2) Ask the child to read the following (in Breakthrough script), taking each sentence in turn.

I see a dog.
I see a television.
I like television.
I like my dog.
I see my dog.
I can see a dog.
I can see my television.
I like my dogs.

(3) Show the child the word *dogs*, printed boldly on a sheet of paper before him. Explain that some words can hide in others by covering the final *s* to leave *dog*, and then the *gs* to leave *do*. If he grasps the idea ask him to find hidden words in the following, taking them one at a time and writing them boldly for him.

      cats   *pink*   *tired*   *redistribute*

Appendix B: Tests Used in the Second Year of Observation (children aged 6 years)

TEST B1

Ask each child to copy the array below on to a sheet of A4 paper.

(Actual dimensions: 1" width for figures in first three rows.
Actual dimensions: ⅝" width for figures in last row.)

TEST B2: LETTER PATTERNS IN WORDS

(The materials used for the questions in this test are taken from the Gay Way Work Book No. 2, *Looking at Words*.)

(1) Show the array below and ask: Can you show me a little word? And another one? Can you show me a big word? And another?

morning	dog	leather
ladybird	window	farmhouse
cat		umbrella
grandmother	children	hen
whiskers	rabbit	boy
pig	birthday	elephant
yellow	scissors	

(2) Show the array below and ask: Can you show me two letters that are the same? And another two that are the same?

star	moon	sun
ship	sheep	gate

(3) Show the array below and, pointing to *st* in *stop*, say: This is *s* (phonic and this is *t*, and together they are *st*. They have a line underneath. Can you find another *st* with a line under, and another? Repeat for *ch* and any other patterns according to response, in each case saying only: Now can you find another like this?

<u>st</u>op	<u>th</u>at	<u>tr</u>ee	<u>tr</u>ap	<u>ch</u>air
<u>sl</u>ot	<u>ch</u>ap	<u>sl</u>ap	<u>st</u>uck	<u>st</u>and
<u>ch</u>ip	<u>st</u>ick	<u>sh</u>ell	<u>tr</u>ain	<u>tr</u>ip
<u>th</u>ey	<u>sl</u>ip	<u>ch</u>uff	<u>th</u>is	<u>sh</u>op
<u>sl</u>eep	<u>sh</u>ed	<u>sh</u>ut	<u>sh</u>e	<u>th</u>e

(4) Show the array below, and cover all words except *must*. Point to its last three letters, covering the *m*, and say that this is a pattern of three letters. Then, covering all other words in the first column and leaving *must* and the right-hand column visible, ask: Can you find another word that has the same pattern of letters at the end? If child is successful, reveal *sat* and ask: Can you find a word that has a pattern at the end like this one? Repeat for other words in first column if useful.

must	Dick
sat	dust
back	ran
sick	rat
can	bud
nest	sack
mud	hill
will	best

(5) Show the array below and point to *oo* in *too*. Say: Here are two letters that are the same, side by side. Can you find two more letters the same, side by side, in another word? Allow repetition to give opportunity for pointing to both *oo* and *ee*.

too	broom	ran	roof
Jack	zoo		sleep
moon		street	boot
see		feet	
shoot	bang		room

(6) Say: I am going to start saying something, but I shall stop before I have finished, or I shall leave a word out. Can you finish it for me or tell me what to say?

With inviting intonation say: *We play with our* ——? If the child supplies a sensible completion, continue with the examples below. If not, try to help so that the examples can then be tried.

> We ride in a ——.
> We eat our ——.
> We —— in a bed.
> We open the ——.
> We —— the ball.
> We —— flowers.
> We put on our ——.
> We live in a ——.
> We like ——.

TEST B3: RETELLING OF STORY 'KANGAROO JOEY FINDS HIS SHADOW' (FROM HEWETT, 1974)

Say to the child that you are going to tell him a story and that you will ask him to tell it back to you in his own way when you have finished. Warn him to listen carefully. Tell the story with such intonation and gesture as maintains interest and attention.

Kangaroo Mother and baby Joey had been playing on the grass. Joey climbed into Mother's pouch to go to sleep. But all at once he saw the shadow. 'Look!' he shouted, pointing a paw. And he nearly fell out of his mother's pocket.

When Kangaroo Mother leapt in the air, the shadow slid on the ground below them, and when she thudded down to the ground the shadow lay still, quietly waiting. 'Slide and stop,' sang Kangaroo Joey. 'Slide and stop. It's following us.' By the time they reached the smoother grass, Kangaroo Joey was wriggling with laughter. 'That shadow has followed us, slide and stop, slide and stop. I think it likes us.'

'I am sure it likes *me*,' said Kangaroo Mother. 'It's my very own shadow. That's why it follows me.' 'Oh!' said Joey. 'I wish it were mine. Can't I borrow it, just for today?' Kangaroo Mother smiled, and said, 'No. It is much too big for you, Joey. You must find your own shadow, to fit your own size. It is waiting for you, there on the grass.' 'I can't see it,' said Kangaroo Joey, screwing up his eyes. 'Where is it?' 'Get out and look,' said Kangaroo Mother.

Joey tumbled out of her pouch, and sat on the patch of sunlit grass. And there behind him, quietly waiting, was a small black shadow, all his own. 'I like it,' said Joey. 'And I think it likes me.' He hopped, and his shadow slid beneath him. Down he came, plop! And his shadow lay still. 'Good! I've got you, shadow,' said Joey. 'You can't get away. I'm sitting on you. Now, come along, shadow. I'm going to hop. Come along, follow me. Come along, shadow.' Kangaroo Joey hopped and plopped, and the shadow slid along and stopped. When Joey ate his dinner, and rested, the shadow lay on the ground beside him. Then Kangaroo Joey hopped again. Hop and plop. Slide and stop. All day long he and his shadow moved across the sunlit grass.

Kangaroo Mother called: 'Time to go home! You and your shadow must go to sleep.' Then Kangaroo Mother and Kangaroo Joey set off side by side towards home, with their very own shadows, one big, one small.

TEST B4: RETELLING OF STORY OF KANGA AND JUMBO (FROM FRANCIS, 1975)

Say to the child that you are going to tell him a story and that you will ask him to tell it back to you in his own way when you have finished. Warn him to listen carefully. Tell the story with such intonation and gesture as maintains interest and attention.

One day Kanga met Jumbo, the elephant, in the High Street of Cuddly Town. Usually Jumbo was very cheerful, but this morning he looked so unhappy that Kanga felt quite worried about him.

'What's the matter, Jumbo?' she asked. Jumbo sniffed. 'I've got to have a tooth out,' he said.

Nobody likes having teeth out, of course, and Kanga knew that. But if you have magic teeth it's rather exciting, and that's what she told him. 'I know someone who always says his teeth are magic,' she said, 'because when he has one out he puts it under his pillow at night, and next morning it has turned into a fivepence.'

Jumbo's face brightened when Kanga told him that. 'How do you know if your teeth are magic?' he asked. Kanga smiled and said, 'You just have to try it and see.'

Jumbo felt very excited as he hurried into the dentist's and he asked for the tooth as soon as it was out. He carried it home in his pocket, wishing it was time for bed. He waited all day long for bed-time, and as soon as he had eaten his tea he ran upstairs and got into bed. Then he put the tooth under his pillow, just as Kanga had told him. A little later Kanga called to see if Jumbo had remembered his tooth. She went upstairs, but he was fast asleep. The tooth was under his pillow when she looked, so she crept downstairs and out of the house as quietly as a mouse.

The very first thing Jumbo did when he woke the next morning was to look under his pillow. There wasn't a sign of his tooth, but exactly where he had put it was a bright, shiny fivepence. He was so pleased he went straight to Kanga's house to tell her all about it.

TEST B5: LANGUAGE IN EXPLANATION AND CONJECTURE

(1) Explanation in dialogue.
Engage the child in an unstructured conversation to explore his understanding of the melting of snow and of its formation.

(2) Use of *because* in sentence completion task, examples being taken of the three classes of *because* sentences described by Piaget (1928).
Say: Can you finish this sentence in a sensible way? (Speak each of the following with an inviting intonation.)

Sentence	Class
I like my friend because . . .	psychological
It gets dark at night because . . .	causal
Mary can't marry Deborah because . . .	logical
The clock stopped because . . .	causal
My dog barked because . . .	psychological
Cats can't fly because . . .	logical

Also say: Can you make up a sentence with *because* in it? (If the child is willing, invite another sentence.)

(3) Use of conjecture.
Say: I am going to ask you some puzzles so you can guess the answers. Let's try one. Yesterday I saw something with two wheels and a saddle. What do you think it was?
If necessary give an answer and try another example. When the child gets the idea try the following:

(*a*) This morning I saw something with two arms and four legs. What do you think I saw? (Suppose child answers *X*.) Do you *know* I saw *X*, or do you *think* I did? Why did you think it was *X*?

(*b*) Repeat with:
There's another thing I saw. It had four legs and a head. What could it have been?

(c) Repeat with:
   Another thing I saw had four legs and a head, but no tail.
   What do you think it was?
   Finally say: I think it might rain later on. What do you think?

(4) Further examples of use of *because*.
   Invite answers to the following questions or prompts:

Questions and prompts	Class
Why can't a dog swallow a horse?	logical
A house can't fit inside a car because . . .	logical
Why did the teacher give one of the children a sweet?	psychological
John hit Peter because . . .	psychological
Why does the light come on when you press the switch?	causal
The man fell off his bicycle because . . .	causal

TEST B6: USE OF 'MORE' AND 'SAME' IN RELATION TO NUMBER

(1) (a) Arrange counters as described in the following moves,
      asking the child to say what is happening at each move.
      Move 1. Align five orange counters in a row.
      Move 2. Match each orange counter with a black one in a
              parallel row.
      Move 3. Spread the orange counters to form a longer row.
      Move 4. Add two black counters to black row, keeping
              total length shorter than orange.
      Move 5. Rearrange black row to equate length with
              orange.
      Move 6. Remove two black counters from end of black
              row.
   (b) Repeat the above moves asking the following questions as
      indicated.
      Move 2. Which row has got more counters than the other?
      Moves 3–6. Now which row has got more counters?

(2) For each of the following comparisons of arrays of counters
   ask the question indicated.
   Same – Is this (pointing) the same as this (pointing)? Why
   (not)?
   More – Which has more counters, this (pointing) or this
   (pointing)? Why?

	Comparison	*Question*
(*a*)	2 with 4, loosely arrayed	Same
(*b*)	5 with 2, loosely arrayed	More
(*c*)	3 with 3, loosely arrayed	Same
(*d*)	2 with 4, loosely arrayed	More
(*e*)	5 with 2, loosely arrayed	Same
(*f*)	3 with 3, loosely arrayed	More
(*g*)	10 with 10, in matched rows	Same
(*h*)	5 with 4, 4 spread more than 5	More
(*i*)	10 with 10, one spread more than other	Same
(*j*)	10 with 10, in matched rows	More
(*k*)	5 with 4, 4 spread more than 5	Same
(*l*)	10 with 10, one spread more than other	More

(3) Arrange two rows of six matchbox trays containing marbles and complete the rows with additional trays and marbles as shown below, for eight different arrays. For each array ask: Are there more marbles in this line? (pointing) or are there more marbles in this line? (again pointing).

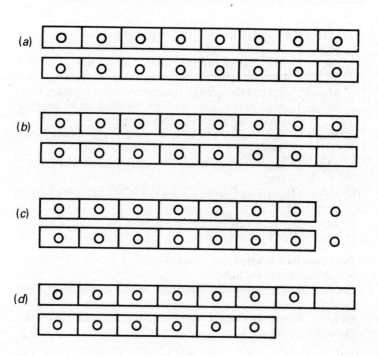

(e)

(f)

(g)

(h)

TEST B7: READING INTERVIEW

(1) Do you like reading?
(2) What do you like about it?
(3) What don't you like about it?
(4) Which book do you like best (*a*) at home, (*b*) at school?
(5) Do you find it easy to remember words?
(6) What do you do to read a word when you can't remember it?
(7) What do you do when you come to a new word?
(8) (*a*) Do pictures help you to read?
    (*b*) How?
(9) (*a*) Does 'sounding' words help you to read?
    (*b*) Does it always work?
    (*c*) When doesn't it work?
(10) (*a*) Does it help if you think of another word that looks like the one you are trying to read?
    (*b*) How does it help?
    (*c*) When doesn't it help?
(11) Do you think reading is useful to children of your age? Why (not)?
(12) How do you think reading could be useful to older children?
(13) How do you think reading could be useful to grown-ups?

(14) Does anybody tell you they want you to be able to read? Who?

(15) (*a*) Does anybody help you to learn to read? Who?

     (*b*) How do they help?

(16) (*a*) Would you like to do more reading in school if you could?

     (*b*) If so, what would you like to do in reading time?

     (*c*) If not, what would you like to do instead of reading?

Appendix C: Tests Used in the Third Year of Observation

TEST C I

After chatting about English and non-English (or foreign) words and the possibility that new English words could be invented or made up if they were needed to name new things, the children were asked to say for each item below – indicated by pointing to it – whether they thought it was real English, made-up English, or foreign. The words were printed in school script. Below is the list in the display presented to the children. They were guided through it row by row. Below again is the classified list.

bed	motting	qap
sitting	wug	thep
thin	tups	bahs
hats	htog	dogs
shup	shot	luds
tiper	rka	driver
dite	came	hopped
teb	cap	fill
tsep	sull	funny
latty	bodl	robbed
migged	ripn	tacn
osk	task	fuller
peller	knud	quick
knob	ftud	happily
sibbily	quop	catch
biggest	metch	vlos
tepped	mabbest	———

		English		Non-English
simple	nonsense	simple with suffix	invented with suffix	
bed	wug	sitting	motting	rka
thin	thep	hats	tups	htog

shot	shup	dogs	luds	bahs
came	dite	driver	tiper	tsep
fill	sull	funny	latty	ripn
cap	teb	hopped	tepped	bodl
task	osk	robbed	migged	tacn
quick	quop	happily	sibbily	qap
knob	knud	fuller	peller	ftud
catch	metch	biggest	mabbest	vlos

TEST C2

Each of the following words was printed in school script on a small card. The children were asked to sort the shuffled cards into one pile of English words and another pile of non-English words. (The terms were again discussed in conversation before the task.)

English	*English nonsense*	*Non-English*
paws	tews	wsib
plug	plen	vopl
help	salp	lpid
swim	swut	dasw
pink	denk	nked
hard	lurd	rdam
drop	dreb	pidr
knob	knid	pakn

TEST C3

After a training task, cancelling the letter *o* systematically row by row and from left to right, the children were given the following passage and asked to cancel all the letters *e* in the same way. They were given copies of the printed version in which print size was similar to that in the Gay Way Violet Book.

Rufty Tufty was a rabbit who wanted to see the world.
'What is the world like?' he said to everyone he met. 'It's a big flat place,' said his mother. 'No, it's square,' said his father, and nobody could agree.
One evening Rufty Tufty saw Wise Old Owl sitting in an oak tree. 'Mr Owl,' he squeaked. 'Can you tell me what the world is like?' The old owl looked wise, then he said, 'The world is round.'
All night Rufty Tufty dreamed of a round world. As soon as he woke up he said 'Good-bye' to his family, and set out to see for himself.

He hadn't gone far – hoppity hop, hoppity hop – when he came to the edge of the woods and saw a fence. Slipping through a gap, Rufty Tufty found himself inside a vegetable garden.

References

Barr, R. (1974), 'The influence of instruction on early reading', *Inter-change*, vol. 5, no. 4, pp. 13–21; also in L. J. Chapman and P. Czerniewska (eds), *Reading: From Process to Practice* (London: Routledge & Kegan Paul, 1978).

Boyce, E. R. (1949), The Gay Way Series (London: Macmillan).

Brimer, M. A., and Dunn, L. M. (1962), *The English Picture Vocabulary Tests* (Bristol: Educational Evaluation Enterprises).

Bryant, P. E., and Bradley, L. (1980), 'Why children sometimes write words which they do not read', in U. Frith (ed.), *Cognitive Processes in Spelling* (London: Academic Press).

Chazan, M., and Williams, P. (1978), *Deprivation and the Infant School* (Oxford: Blackwell).

Clark, M. M. (1976), *Young Fluent Readers* (London: Heinemann).

Clay, M. (1969), 'Reading errors and self-correction behaviour', *British Journal of Educational Psychology*, vol. 39, pt 1, pp. 47–56.

Clay, M. (1972), *Reading: The Patterning of Complex Behaviour* (London: Heinemann).

Cohen, J. (1979), 'Patterns of parental help', *Educational Research,* vol. 21, no. 3, pp. 186–93.

Coltheart, M. (1978), 'Lexical access in simple reading tasks', in G. Underwood (ed.), *Strategies of Information Processing* (London: Academic Press).

Daniels, J. C., and Diack, H. (1958), *The Standard Reading Tests* (London: Chatto & Windus).

Donaldson, M. (1978), *Children's Minds* (Glasgow: Fontana/Collins).

Downing, J. (1970), 'Children's concepts of language in learning to read', *Educational Research*, vol. 12, no. 2, pp. 106–12.

Downing, J. (1979), *Reading and Reasoning* (Edinburgh: Chambers).

Durkin, D. (1961), 'Children who read before grade one', *The Reading Teacher,* vol. 14 (November), pp. 163–6.

Durkin, D. (1962), 'Reading instruction and the five-year-old child', in *Challenge and Experiment in Reading* (New York: Scholastic Magazines).

Francis, H. (1973), 'Children's experience of reading and notions of units in language', *British Journal of Educational Psychology*, vol. 43, pt 1, pp. 17–23.

Francis, H. (1975), *Language in Childhood* (London: Elek).

Francis, H. (1977), 'Children's strategies in learning to read', *British Journal of Educational Psychology*, vol. 47 pt 2, pp. 117–25.

Gibson, E. J., and Levin, H. (1975), *The Psychology of Reading* (Cambridge, Mass.: MIT Press).

Harris, D. B. (1963), *Children's Drawings as Measures of Intellectual Maturity* (New York: Harcourt, Brace & World).

Henderson, L., and Chard, J. (1980), 'The reader's implicit knowledge of orthographic structure', in U. Frith (ed.), *Cognitive Processes in Spelling* (London: Academic Press).

Hewett, A. (1974), *The Anita Hewett Animal Story Book* (Harmondsworth: Penguin/Puffin).

Hewison, J., and Tizard, J. (1980), 'Parental involvement and reading attainment', *British Journal of Educational Psychology*, vol. 50, pt 3, pp. 209–15.

Krippner, S. (1963), 'The boy who read at eighteen months', *Exceptional Children*, vol. 30 (October), pp. 105–9.

Mackay, D., Thompson, B., and Schaub, P. (1970), *Breakthrough to Literacy: Teacher's Manual* (London: Longman).

MacKinnon, A. R. (1959), *How Do Children Learn To Read?* (Vancouver: Copp Clark).

Piaget, J. (1928), *Judgment and Reasoning in the Child* (London: Routledge & Kegan Paul).

Pidgeon, D. (1976), 'Logical steps in the process of learning to read', *Educational Research,* vol. 18, no. 3, pp. 174–81.

Reid, J. (1966), 'Learning to think about reading', *Educational Research,* vol. 9, no. 1, pp. 56–62.

Schonell, F. J. (1945), *The Psychology and Teaching of Reading* (Edinburgh: Oliver & Boyd).

Soderbergh, R. (1971), *Reading in Early Childhood* (Stockholm: Almqvist & Wiksell).

Stubbs, M. (1980), *Language and Literacy* (London: Routledge & Kegan Paul).

Vygotsky, L. S. (1962), *Thought and Language* (Cambridge, Mass.: MIT Press).

Young, D. (1968), *Group Reading Test* (London: Hodder & Stoughton).

Index